Contents

Introduction

Body Confidence is Volume 307 in the **ISSUES** series. The aim of the series is to offer current, diverse information about important issues in our world, from a UK perspective.

ABOUT BODY CONFIDENCE

With children as young as six suffering from body image issues, body confidence and self-esteem are highly debated topics. This book considers topics such as the impact of selfies on young people's confidence, Body Dysmorphic Disorder, mental health and body image and plastic surgery. It also explores ways of improving self-esteem, and both the positive and negative effects of social media.

OUR SOURCES

Titles in the **ISSUES** series are designed to function as educational resource books, providing a balanced overview of a specific subject.

The information in our books is comprised of facts, articles and opinions from many different sources, including:

⇨ Newspaper reports and opinion pieces

⇨ Website factsheets

⇨ Magazine and journal articles

⇨ Statistics and surveys

⇨ Government reports

⇨ Literature from special interest groups.

A NOTE ON CRITICAL EVALUATION

Because the information reprinted here is from a number of different sources, readers should bear in mind the origin of the text and whether the source is likely to have a particular bias when presenting information (or when conducting their research). It is hoped that, as you read about the many aspects of the issues explored in this book, you will critically evaluate the information presented.

It is important that you decide whether you are being presented with facts or opinions. Does the writer give a biased or unbiased report? If an opinion is being expressed, do you agree with the writer? Is there potential bias to the 'facts' or statistics behind an article?

ASSIGNMENTS

In the back of this book, you will find a selection of assignments designed to help you engage with the articles you have been reading and to explore your own opinions. Some tasks will take longer than others and there is a mixture of design, writing and research-based activities that you can complete alone or in a group.

FURTHER RESEARCH

At the end of each article we have listed its source and a website that you can visit if you would like to conduct your own research. Please remember to critically evaluate any sources that you consult and consider whether the information you are viewing is accurate and unbiased.

Useful weblinks

www.baaps.org.uk

www.bddfoundation.org

www.bustle.com

ceop.police.uk

www.commonsensemedia.org

www.ditchthelabel.org

www.gov.uk

www.huffingtonpost.co.uk

www.leedsbeckett.ac.uk

www.mind.org.uk

www.nedc.com.au/body-image

www.nhs.uk

www.nuffieldbioethics.org

www.parentinfo.org

www.telegraph.co.uk

www.theconversation.com

www.theguardian.com

www.thirdforcenews.org.uk

unh.edu

www.yougov.co.uk

MidKent College
LEARNING RESOURCE CENTRE

Medway Campus

Class No: _____ 158·1 _____

ACR

Return on or before the date last stamped below:

For renewals phone 01634 383044

Independence Educational Publishers

First published by Independence Educational Publishers

The Studio, High Green

Great Shelford

Cambridge CB22 5EG

England

© Independence 2016

ISBN-13: 978 1 86168 752 4

Printed in Great Britain
Zenith Print Group

What is body image?

Body image is the perception that a person has of their physical self and the thoughts and feelings that result from that perception.

These feelings can be positive, negative or both and are influenced by individual and environmental factors.

The four aspects of body image:

1. How you see your body is your perceptual body image. This is not always a correct representation of how you actually look. For example, a person may perceive themselves as overweight when they are actually underweight.

2. The way you feel about your body is your affective body image. This relates to the amount of satisfaction or dissatisfaction you feel about your shape, weight and individual body parts.

3. The way you think about your body is your cognitive body image. This can lead to preoccupation with body shape and weight. For example, some people believe they will feel better about themselves if they are thinner or more muscular.

4. Behaviours in which you engage as a result of your body image encompass your behavioural body image. When a person is dissatisfied with the way they look, they may isolate themselves because they feel bad about their appearance or employ destructive behaviours (e.g. excessive exercising, disordered eating) as a means to change appearance.

Why is positive body image important?

Positive body image occurs when a person is able to accept, appreciate and respect their body. Positive body image is important because it is one of the protective factors which can make a person more resilient to eating disorders.

In fact, the most effective eating disorder prevention programmes use a health promotion approach, focusing on building self-esteem and positive body image, and a balanced approach to nutrition and physical activity. A positive body image will improve:

⇨ **Self-esteem**, which dictates how a person feels about themselves and can infiltrate every aspect of life, and contribute to happiness and wellbeing.

⇨ **Self-acceptance**, making a person more likely to feel comfortable and happy with the way they look and less likely to feel impacted by unrealistic images in the media and societal pressures to look a certain way.

⇨ **Healthy outlook and behaviours**, as it is easier to lead a balanced lifestyle with healthier attitudes and practices relating to food and exercise when you are in tune with, and respond to the needs of your body.

What causes body dissatisfaction?

When a person has negative thoughts and feelings about his or her own body, body dissatisfaction can develop. Body dissatisfaction is an internal process but can be influenced by several external factors. For example, family, friends, acquaintances, teachers and the media all have an impact on how a person sees and feels about themselves and their appearance. Individuals in appearance-oriented environments or those who receive negative feedback about their appearance are at an increased risk of body dissatisfaction.

One of the most common external contributors to body dissatisfaction is the media. People of all ages are bombarded with images through TV, magazines, Internet and advertising. These images often promote unrealistic, unobtainable and highly stylised appearance ideals which have been fabricated by stylists, art teams and digital manipulation and cannot be achieved in real life. Those who feel they don't measure up in comparison to these images, can experience intense body dissatisfaction which is damaging to their psychological and physical wellbeing.

The following factors make some people more likely to develop a negative body image than others:

⇨ **Age** – body image is frequently shaped during late childhood and adolescence but body dissatisfaction can affect people of all ages and is as prevalent in midlife as young adulthood in women

⇨ **Gender** – adolescent girls are more prone to body dissatisfaction than adolescent boys; however, the rate of body dissatisfaction in males is rapidly approaching that of females

⇨ **Low self-esteem and/or depression**

⇨ **Personality traits** – people with perfectionist tendencies, high achievers, 'black and white' thinkers, those who internalise beauty ideals, and those who often compare themselves to others, are at higher risk of developing body dissatisfaction

⇨ **Teasing** – people who are teased about appearance/ weight, regardless of actual body type, have an increased risk of developing body dissatisfaction

⇨ **Friends and family who diet and express body image concerns** – role models expressing body image concerns and modelling weight loss behaviours, can increase the likelihood of an individual developing body dissatisfaction regardless of actual body type

⇨ **Body size** – In our weight-conscious society, larger body size increases risk of body dissatisfaction.

In western society, body dissatisfaction has become a cultural norm.

Why is body dissatisfaction a serious problem?

Body dissatisfaction is the top ranked issue of concern for young people, according to Mission Australia (2011). Body image issues have increased worldwide over the last 30 years and do not only concern young people but affect people of all ages. This pervasive problem is concerning because overvaluing body image in defining one's self-worth is one of the risk factors which makes some people less resilient to eating disorders than others. People experiencing body dissatisfaction can become fixated on trying to change their body shape, which can lead to unhealthy practices with food and exercise. These practices don't usually achieve the desired outcome (physically or emotionally) and can result in intense feelings of disappointment, shame and guilt and, ultimately, increase the risk of developing an eating disorder.

How can you improve your body image?

While some aspects of your appearance can be changed, others, like your height, muscle composition and bone structure are genetically fixed. It is important to understand that there is no right or wrong when it comes to weight, shape, size and appearance. Challenging beauty ideals and learning to accept your body shape is a crucial step towards positive body image.

While changing your actual appearance can be counterproductive, improving your body image is a constructive goal. We have the power to change the way we see, feel and think about our bodies. Here are some helpful tips:

⇨ Focusing on your positive qualities, skills and talents can help you accept and appreciate your whole self

⇨ Say positive things to yourself every day

⇨ Avoid negative or berating self-talk

⇨ Focusing on appreciating and respecting what your body can do will help you to feel more positively about it

⇨ Setting positive, health-focused goals rather than weight loss-related ones is more beneficial for your overall wellbeing

⇨ Admiring others' beauty can improve your own body confidence but it is important to appreciate your own beauty, avoid comparing yourself to others, accept yourself as a whole and remember that everyone is unique and differences are what make us special

⇨ Remember, many media images are unrealistic and represent a minority of the population.

Programmes that effectively increase positive body image focus on reducing risk factors (e.g. thin ideal internalisation, peer pressure, bullying and 'fat talk', perfectionism) and increasing protective factors (e.g. self-esteem, social support, non-competitive physical activity, healthy eating behaviours and attitudes, respect for diversity).

Getting help

If you feel dissatisfied with your body or are developing unhealthy eating or exercise habits seek professional help. Some counsellors and psychologists have specialised knowledge in body image. Professional support can help guide you to change negative beliefs and behaviours.

⇨ The above information is reprinted with kind permission from the National Eating Disorders Collaboration. Please visit www.nedc.com.au/body-image for further information.

Children as young as six suffering body image problems

By Carrie Braithwaite

Research presented by Professor Pinki Sahota and colleagues from our University's Institute for Health & Wellbeing at this year's European Congress on Obesity, in Prague, shows that children as young as six and seven years old (Year 2 in the UK school system) are suffering dissatisfaction with their body shape.

"Results showed that children categorised as overweight had higher body shape dissatisfaction scores on average than normal weight children"

Few studies have analysed the association between psychological wellbeing and body mass index (BMI) in young children under nine years old. In this new research, led by Professor Sahota, with Dr Meaghan Christian and Dr Rhiannon Day at Leeds Beckett and Kim Cocks of KCStats Consultancy, describe the association of psychological wellbeing (dieting behaviours and body image perception) and BMI in primary school children from Year 2 (age six–seven years) and Year 4 (age eight–nine years).

Data was collected from 301 pupils (52% boys) from eight primary schools in Leeds, participating in the Phunky Foods feasibility study – an early years and primary school programme of healthy lifestyle activities. Psychological wellbeing was measured using the Body Shape Perception Scale and the Measure of Dieting Behaviours (modified version of the Dutch Eating Behaviour Questionnaire).

A total of 59 (19%) of the 301 children in the study were overweight or obese. The results showed that children categorised as overweight (85th to 95th percentile) or obese

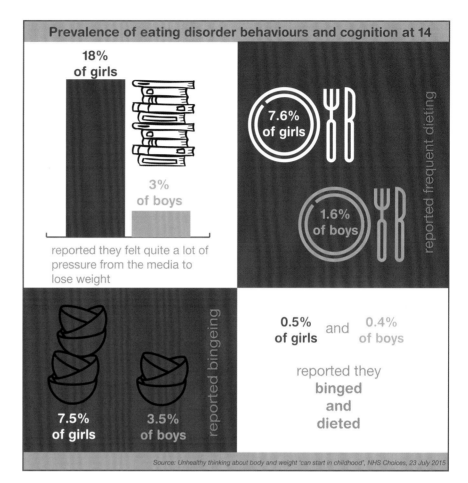

Prevalence of eating disorder behaviours and cognition at 14

18% of girls / 3% of boys — reported they felt quite a lot of pressure from the media to lose weight

7.6% of girls / 1.6% of boys — reported frequent dieting

7.5% of girls / 3.5% of boys — reported bingeing

0.5% of girls and 0.4% of boys — reported they binged and dieted

Source: Unhealthy thinking about body and weight 'can start in childhood', NHS Choices, 23 July 2015

(>=95th percentile) using the World Health Organization (WHO) BMI Growth Charts had higher body shape dissatisfaction scores on average than normal weight children.

Girls had higher body shape dissatisfaction scores, showing that girls had a higher desire to be thinner than boys. Scores related to dietary restraint (dieting behaviours) showed that overweight and obese pupils reported more dietary restraint than their normal weight peers. Younger children aged six–seven years also reported more dietary restraint than those aged eight–nine years. Dietary restraint means that children are exhibiting dieting behaviours which may lead to compromising the quality of the diet at a time when they need a good quality, healthy diet for growth and development.

Professor Sahota concluded: "The results suggested that body shape dissatisfaction and dietary restraint behaviours may begin in children as young as six and seven years old, and there is an association with increased BMI. Obesity prevention programmes need to consider psychological wellbeing and ensure that it is not compromised. Further research should be conducted on how interventions can help improve psychological wellbeing in this age group."

7 May 2015

⇨ The above information is reprinted with kind permission from Leeds Beckett University. Please visit www.leedsbeckett.ac.uk for further information.

© Leeds Beckett University 2016

Women's body confidence is a "critical issue" worldwide, warns Dove's largest ever report

Almost 70% women feel the media drives their appearance anxiety.

By Rachel Moss, Lifestyle Writer at The Huffington Post UK

Women's body confidence has become a "critical issue" around the world and pressure from the media is largely to blame for our low self-esteem, a new report warns.

The *Dove Global Beauty and Confidence Report*, given exclusively to The Huffington Post UK, has been created using interviews with 10,500 women and girls across 13 countries and is the largest the brand has ever commissioned.

It found that women in the UK have one of the lowest body confidence scores in the world, with only 20% of us saying we like the way that we look.

Globally, more than two-thirds of women (69%) and girls (65%) say increasing pressures from advertising and media to reach an unrealistic standard of beauty is the key force in driving their appearance anxiety.

Meanwhile, 56% of all women recognise the impact of an "always on" social media culture in driving the pressure for perfection and negative body image.

The report reveals that low body esteem is causing the majority of women (85%) and girls (79%) to opt out of important life activities – such as trying out for a team or club, and engaging with family or loved ones – when they don't feel good about the way they look.

Additionally, seven in ten girls with low body esteem say they won't be assertive in their opinion or stick to their decision if they aren't happy with the way they look, while nine out of ten (87%) women will stop themselves from eating or will otherwise put their health at risk.

What's more, nearly eight in 10 (78%) of both women and girls feel some pressure to never make mistakes or show weakness.

"This latest research shows that low body confidence is a global issue," says Dr Nancy Etcoff of Harvard Medical School.

"Though troubling, these results are also unsurprising, given the increasing pressures women and girls face today.

"We need to help empower women and girls in many ways, including increasing body-confidence education, driving meaningful conversations around the pressures women and girls face, and advocating for change in how females and their appearance are talked about and portrayed in the media."

The report found that beauty and appearance anxiety is a global issue, but one that women are experiencing differently by culture and country.

While women in South Africa are the most body confident with 64% saying they have "high body esteem", women in the UK come in 12th out of 13 countries, with only 20% of us saying we feel good about the way we look.

But it's not all bad news for women and girls when it comes to body image.

The report reveals there is a proactive desire among females to challenge existing beauty norms.

A total of 71% of women and 67% of girls want to call on the media to do a better job portraying women of diverse physical appearance, age, race, shape and size.

Additionally, while 60% of women believe they need to meet certain beauty standards, at the same time, 77% agree it is important to be their own person and not copy anyone else.

For many women and girls, the key to breaking a cycle of beauty and appearance anxiety seems to be the experience of taking time to care for their minds, body and appearance.

In fact, seven in ten women and eight in ten girls report feeling more confident or positive when they invest time in caring for themselves.

"Taking time for care – whether it's body or mind – is an important step in improving the confidence of women and girls," says Victoria Sjardin, senior global director of Dove Masterbrand.

"For over 50 years, Dove has been committed to creating a world where beauty is a source of confidence, not anxiety.

"With this new research, we hope to inspire women and girls everywhere to develop a positive relationship with the way they look."

21 June 2016

⇨ The above information is reprinted with kind permission from The Huffington Post UK. Please visit www.huffingtonpost.co.uk for further information.

Over a third of Brits are unhappy with their bodies

As part of a global study from YouGov, it has been revealed that over a third of people in the UK are unhappy with their own weight and body image, although those in the oldest age group are by far the happiest.

The study captured the body image happiness of people in 25 countries around the world. In Britain, over a third (37%) said they were either not very happy or not happy at all with their body image and weight. 59% said they were happy.

There is a gender split. Woman are far more likely to be unhappy with their body image. Over four in ten (44%) are not happy, compared to 53% who are. Men seem to be a little bit more comfortable in their own skin – 66% are happy compared to 31% that are not.

Does loving your body begin at 60? Certainly the sexagenarians in our poll liked their bodies more than other age groups. Almost seven in ten (68%) of 60+ are happy, compared to 52% of 25–39-year-olds.

What about the rest of the world?

While a fair number of people are unhappy with their bodies in the UK, people are more positive elsewhere. Of the 25 countries surveyed, Indonesians are the most positive about their body image overall, with more than three quarters (78%) claiming they are happy with their body weight and shape. Residents from Saudi Arabia (72%), Oman (70%) and Qatar (70%) are the next happiest with their body image overall.

However, those in Hong Kong are the least happy, and it is the only country where net happiness is below half (49%).

Celebrity culture

So what is the cause of so many people being unhappy with their weight? According to our global respondents, celebrity culture is one of the areas of blame. In the UK, almost three quarters (74%) say that celebrity culture has a negative impact on women's perception of their bodies, while the same number say it affects young people in the same way. Overall, in 17 of the 25 countries surveyed more than half of responders think that celebrity culture has a negative impact on young people.

The countries surveyed in the Middle East and Asia Pacific have a more positive view of the impact of celebrity culture on young people. Around a third in the UAE (34%) and Qatar (31%) think celebrity culture can have a positive effect, along with 41% in mainland China and over one in three (34%) in Malaysia and Thailand.

21 July 2015

⇨ The above information is reprinted with kind permission from YouGov. Please visit www.yougov.co.uk for further information.

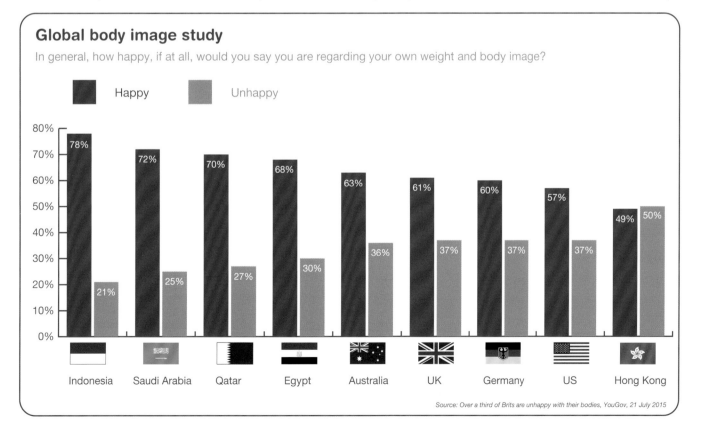

Global body image study

In general, how happy, if at all, would you say you are regarding your own weight and body image?

Legend: ■ Happy ▨ Unhappy

Country	Happy	Unhappy
Indonesia	78%	21%
Saudi Arabia	72%	25%
Qatar	70%	27%
Egypt	68%	30%
Australia	63%	36%
UK	61%	37%
Germany	60%	37%
US	57%	37%
Hong Kong	49%	50%

Source: Over a third of Brits are unhappy with their bodies, YouGov, 21 July 2015

Selfies: the good, the bad and the downright irritating

The selfie has become a huge part of modern life. It has transformed the simple self-portrait into something more immediate and has grown in cultural importance – it's been linked to identity, self-exploration and narcissism. Something as simple as putting a camera on the front of a mobile device has created a cultural trend that looks set to last.

Fears about the impact of the selfie generation were recently brought to the fore with the story of Essena O'Neill – the popular Instagrammer who claimed she quit the platform after her online presence started to impact negatively on her life. So is it something to worry about, or just a bit of harmless fun?

By Lucy Doyle

Selfies are everywhere. In 2013 it was named word of the year by Oxford Dictionaries, in 2014 a song was released called #selfie,[1] selfie sticks were banned in Disneyland in July 2015 and you could argue that the world would be seeing a lot less of Kim Kardashian and her clan if the selfie had never been invented.

Recent figures show that 91% of teens have taken a selfie and over one million are taken each day.[2]

Let's get it right: sexting vs selfies

Sometimes the actions of 'sexting' (sending sexually explicit words, videos or images to somebody, known as 'nude selfies' and 'nudes') and sending someone a selfie become confused. Sending a selfie only moves into the territory of 'sexting' when a naked, suggestive or sexualised image is sent.

A selfie, on the other hand, normally refers to a non-sexual self-portrait, taken on a mobile device, either with friends or alone. It may or may not involve at least one of the people featured making a 'duck face' at the camera.

Narcissism

Some people worry that selfies are helping to create a superficial generation who value their looks above anything else.

People's growing obsession with posting the perfect selfie is evident in the existence of apps designed to allow the user to touch up and perfect their image before posting online.

Posting selfies online has also been linked to self-objectification, which is when you view your body as an object based on its sexual value, and tend to derive your sense of self-worth from appearance.

Many worry that such focus on looks can undermine young people's self-confidence and body image. Young people can get caught up in how they're portrayed on social media; seeking approval and affirmation from others in the form of likes and retweets. Relying too heavily on this as a means of boosting self-esteem will inevitably lead to unhappiness and low self-confidence when they're not getting as much praise and approval online as they'd like.

This appeared to be the case with Essena O'Neill – the teen famous for her incredibly popular social media presence, particularly on Instagram. In November 2015, she famously quit the platform, stating how social media wasn't real, that the focus on gaining likes and followers had made her feel "miserable" and that it was simply "contrived perfection to get attention".

"When you let yourself be defined by numbers, you let yourself be defined by something that is not pure,"[3] she said.

She added new captions to her photos, stating the truth behind them: many were PR shots and it often took hours to get that "this is me just hanging out" look just right.

Psychologist Dr Linda Papadopoulos has described how young people can get too caught up in their online presence, which tends to be more about gaining status and approval than individuality. This can result in young people being unsure of who they truly are as a person.

Dr Papadopoulos encourages young people to be aware of this and to take time to foster an offline, real sense of self and identity, while also relying less on their online profile as a means of defining who they are.

Selfies on social media

Several separate studies have shown that an image-centric social media platform, such as Facebook, can cause depressive symptoms. This is because of the way Facebook enables and encourages the user to compare themselves to others.[4]

Some people go to extraordinary lengths to curate the 'perfect' online persona. They remove or de-tag any unflattering pictures, only the most attractive selfies are posted, and the only moments which are recorded are the positive or happy ones, creating the illusion of a flawless existence.

When young people forget that this isn't real, and compare their entire self, complete with flaws and down days, to other people's curated, perfected versions of themselves, they can start to feel inferior and as though they fall short of everyone else.[5]

It's really important to remind young people that comparing themselves to others on social media is unhelpful, as they're comparing themselves to something impossible and unattainable – nobody looks fantastic all the time and everyone has bad days.

As long as young people are aware of this, they can make the most out of all the benefits of social media – staying in touch with friends, posting photos and organising social events.

Selfies with friends

A study at the University of Georgia identified three main reasons people take selfies: self-absorption, art and a social connection. For most young people, the latter will be the reason they're taking a selfie.

Taking a selfie, maybe pulling a silly face, and sending it to a friend is an amusing, unique way to communicate. Also, taking selfies within a group of friends is a great way to bond, cement friendships and create memories.

There's no need to panic about your child becoming self-obsessed if they spend quite a bit of time posing for selfies with friends, or on their own. Teenagers are naturally preoccupied with how they look as they change and grow – this has always been a natural part of teen life. Selfies have given them a new way of expressing this, and it's likely they'll grow out of any slightly worrying predilection towards taking too many of them.

Selfie safety

There have been several worrying reports of children taking inappropriate selfies that then end up in the wrong hands. This has led to a panic around the subject of selfies and children.

But, taking a selfie rarely falls into the category of sexting, and starting a conversation about selfies with your child provides a good opportunity to raise the importance of their online reputation.

Remind them that what goes online stays online, and when they post a selfie, or send one to a friend, boyfriend or girlfriend, the image is then out of their control.

If they're unsure about sending it because it's embarrassing, a little

bit too silly, or perhaps rather risqué, it's always best not to. Have a look at our article on digital reputation for more information.

For advice on what to do if your child has sent someone a selfie they regret taking, or if it's been shared online.

The verdict

In the vast majority of cases, selfies are fun and harmless. The only time you may need to intervene is if your child's selfie-taking is leading to them becoming overly-concerned about their appearance, it's affecting their self-confidence or if they've sent someone a picture they regret taking.

Doing anything in excess isn't good, but as long as you encourage your child to lead a balanced life, then selfies will simply be another way to have fun in the digital age.

References

1. https://www.youtube.com/watch?v=kdemFfbS5H0

2. http://socialmediaweek.org/blog/2014/08/selfie-boom-good-bad-selfies-will-change-future/

3. http://www.theguardian.com/media/2015/nov/03/instagram-star-essena-oneill-quits-2d-life-to-reveal-true-story-behind-images

4. http://guilfordjournals.com/doi/abs/10.1521/jscp.2014.33.8.701

5. http://guilfordjournals.com/doi/abs/10.1521/jscp.2014.33.8.701

⇨ The above information is reprinted with kind permission from Parent Zone and CEOP. Please visit www.parentinfo.org for further information.

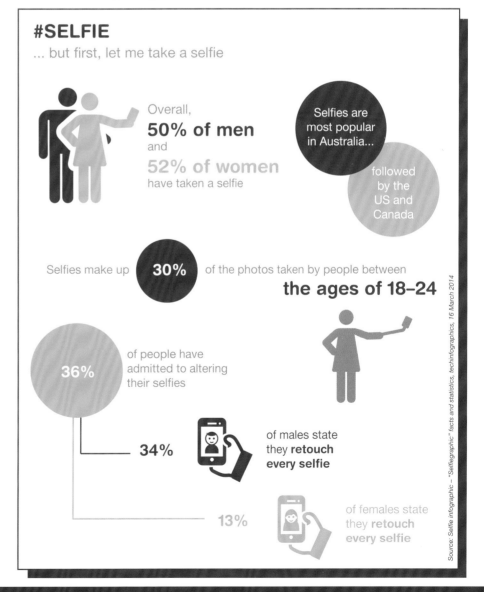

#SELFIE
... but first, let me take a selfie

Overall, **50% of men** and **52% of women** have taken a selfie

Selfies are most popular in Australia... followed by the US and Canada

Selfies make up **30%** of the photos taken by people between **the ages of 18–24**

36% of people have admitted to altering their selfies

34% of males state they **retouch every selfie**

13% of females state they **retouch every selfie**

Source: Selfie infographic – "Selfiegraphic" facts and statistics, techinfographics, 16 March 2014

Body Dysmorphic Disorder (BDD)

About BDD

Body Dysmorphic Disorder (BDD) is characterised by a preoccupation with one or more perceived defects or flaws in appearance, which is unnoticeable to others. Sometimes the flaw is noticeable but is a normal variation (e.g. male pattern baldness) or is not as prominent as the sufferer believes.

The older term for BDD is 'dysmorphophobia', which is sometimes still used. The media sometimes refer to BDD as "Imagined Ugliness Syndrome". This isn't particularly helpful as the ugliness is very real to the individual concerned, and does not reflect the severe distress that BDD can cause.

As well as the excessive self-consciousness, individuals with BDD often feel defined by their flaw. They often experience an image of their perceived defect associated with memories, emotions and bodily sensations – as if seeing the flaw through the eyes of an onlooker, even though what they 'see' may be very different to their appearance observed by others. Sufferers tend repeatedly to check on how bad their flaw is (for example in mirrors and reflective surfaces), attempt to camouflage or alter the perceived defect and avoid public or social situations or triggers that increase distress. They may at times be housebound or have needless cosmetic and dermatological treatments. There is no doubt that the symptoms cause significant distress or handicap and there is an increased risk of suicide and attempted suicide.

What if I have a 'real' defect?

People with BDD often ask this question. The key is to understand that BDD is a problem of excessive worry and shame about appearance that will persist despite reassurance. It is often associated with fears of rejection or humiliation. Some sufferers acknowledge that they may be blowing things out of proportion. Others are so firmly convinced about their defect that they do not believe others (for example family members,

friends or health professionals) trying to reassure them that it is unnoticeable or unimportant.

Whatever the degree of insight into their condition, sufferers are likely to have been told that they look "normal" many times. They have often been teased or bullied in the past about their appearance (e.g. acne, "big ears") but this probably reflects far more about the bully than their target. Furthermore their appearance has usually changed since the teasing began.

A 'real' defect such as a facial disfigurement that others can easily notice can also cause marked distress. You may not have BDD but you can still be helped to feel and function better – see for example www.changingfaces.org.uk.

When does concern with appearance become BDD?

Many of us are concerned with some aspect of our appearance but to amount to BDD the preoccupation must last for at least an hour a day, cause significant distress and/or interfere with at least one area of life. For example, some people with BDD avoid social and public situations to prevent feelings of discomfort and worry about being rated negatively by those around them.

Instead, they may enter such situations but remain very self-conscious. They may use excessive camouflage to hide their perceived defect – heavy make-up perhaps, or a change of posture, a particular hair style or heavy clothes. They may spend several hours a day thinking about their perceived defect and asking themselves questions that cannot be answered (for example, "Why was I born this way?" "If only my nose was straighter and smaller").

People with BDD may feel compelled to repeat certain time-consuming behaviours such as:

⇨ Checking their appearance in a mirror or reflective surface

⇨ Checking by feeling their skin with their fingers

⇨ Cutting or combing their hair to make it 'just so'

⇨ Picking their skin to make it smooth

⇨ Comparing themselves against models in magazines or people in the street

⇨ Discuss their appearance with others

⇨ Camouflaging their appearance.

People with BDD may also avoid certain places, people, or activities because of concerns over their appearance (e.g. bright lights, mirrors, dating, social situations, being seen close up).

These behaviours all make sense if you feel you look ugly as they are designed to make you feel safe (for example, camouflage) or to determine whether you look as bad as you think you do (for example, checking in a mirror). However, they lead to an increase in preoccupation and distress with your appearance.

How does BDD affect emotion?

The kinds of emotional distress that the preoccupation of BDD can cause includes:

⇨ Anxiety

⇨ Shame

⇨ Depression

⇨ Disgust.

Even if a sufferer's concern about their appearance is not noticeable to others excessive, their distress is very real.

What are the effects of BDD on life?

By definition, the impact of BDD on a person's quality of life is going to be significant, but it can be severe. Some individuals end up with lives so limited that they effectively become housebound. Many sufferers are single or divorced which suggests that they find it difficult to form or maintain relationships.

BDD at its worst can make regular employment or family life impossible. Those in regular employment or who have family responsibilities would almost certainly find life more productive and satisfying if they did not have the symptoms of BDD. Partners, friends and family members find it very distressing when they are unable to help the person they love stop feeling ugly and regain control of their lives.

Which parts of the body are involved in BDD?

Most people with BDD are preoccupied with some aspect of their face and many believe they have multiple defects. The most common complaints (in descending order) concern the skin, nose, hair, eyes, chin, lips and the overall body build. People with BDD may complain of a lack of symmetry, or feel that something is too big, too small, or out of proportion to the rest of the body. Any part of the body may be involved in BDD including the breasts or genitals.

Muscle dysmorphia

'Muscle dysmorphia' is the term sometimes used to describe BDD in which the person is preoccupied with muscle size, shape and leanness. People with muscle dysmorphia often believe that they look 'puny' or 'small', when in reality they look normal or may even be more muscular than average. This can then lead to preoccupation with diet (e.g. very high protein supplements) and life can end up revolving around workouts.

Some damage their health by excessively working out and others report use of anabolic steroids in an attempt to increase lean muscle. Similar to other presentations of BDD, there are other repetitive behaviours (e.g. camouflaging with clothing to make one's body appear larger, mirror checking, reassurance checking). Sufferers then neglect important social or occupational activities because of shame over their perceived appearance flaws and the amount of time taken up by their appearance-related activities.

Are people with BDD vain?

No! People with BDD believe themselves to be ugly or defective. They tend to be very secretive and reluctant to seek help because they are afraid that others will think them vain or narcissistic. People with BDD are quite the opposite from being vain or deliberately self-obsessed; BDD is a serious disorder that affects at least one per cent of the population. It shares similarities with obsessive-compulsive disorder, health anxiety and social phobia.

BDD affects men and women equally, and most commonly begins in adolescence. Because of the stigma attached to BDD and the current poor level of awareness, on average a person with BDD will suffer for ten years before seeking help.

BDD by proxy

BDD by proxy is a little known variant of BDD in which an aspect or aspects of another person's appearance are the focus of preoccupation. Most commonly the other person is the sufferer's partner or child. People with BDD by proxy have often had BDD or OCD themselves at some time.

In many ways the behaviours (checking, comparing, avoidance and so on) in BDD by proxy are similar to those of 'self-focused' BDD and it can cause hours of preoccupation and great distress. There has been relatively little research in this area, but clinical experience has shown that the same treatment approach used for 'self-focused' BDD can be effective for BDD by proxy.

How common is BDD?

BDD usually develops in adolescence, a time when people are generally most sensitive about their appearance. However, many sufferers leave it for 15 years before seeking appropriate help. They are most likely to consult dermatologists or cosmetic practitioners. When they do seek help through mental health professionals, they often present with other symptoms such as depression, social anxiety or obsessive-compulsive disorder and do not reveal their real concerns. Therefore, it is not easy to know what proportion of the population suffers from BDD.

It is recognised as a hidden disorder as many people with BDD are too ashamed to reveal their main problem. Surveys have put BDD at about 2% of the population. It is more common in adolescents and young people. We know very little about cultural influences in BDD – for example, it may be more common in cultures that put an emphasis on the importance of appearance. In the West, it is equally common in men and women although milder BDD may be more common in women.

Are there any differences between men and women with BDD?

There are more similarities than differences between men and women with BDD. However, men may be more concerned about their genitals, body build, and thinning or balding hair. Women may be more concerned with skin, stomach, weight, breasts, buttocks, thighs, legs, hips and excessive body hair. Women are more likely to check mirrors excessively, change their clothes and pick their skin whereas men are more likely to lift weights excessively.

It must be nice being a dog and not having to fuss about how you look.

What is the typical course of BDD?

BDD usually begins in late adolescence (16–18 years). However, milder symptoms of BDD often precede this from about the age of 12–14. However, it may take up to 15 years before presentation to mental health professionals.

What causes BDD?

There has been very little research into BDD, which urgently needs funding so that we can understand it fully and develop better treatments.

There may be a genetic predisposition or vulnerability to the disorder, which would make a person more likely to develop BDD in certain situations. Thus some people with BDD may have a relative with BDD, OCD or depression. Thus poor attachment to a carer and certain stresses during adolescence such as teasing, bullying or abuse may make the person more vulnerable.

For some, perfectionism may be a factor but it is not generally true of people with BDD. They may, however, appreciate aesthetics more in their self or others and have had training or interest in art or design.

Once BDD has started, it is maintained by the way a person judges themselves almost exclusively by their 'felt impression' or what they see in a mirror. This image may be like a ghost from the past, for example, when they were teased or rejected. The person with BDD may fear being alone and isolated all their life or being worthless. Once the disorder has developed it can be maintained by excessive self-focus, rumination, avoidance behaviours, and excessive checking, comparison and reassurance seeking.

⇨ The above information is reprinted with kind permission from the Body Dysmorphic Disorder Foundation. Please visit www.bddfoundation.org for further information.

© Body Dysmorphic Disorder Foundation 2016

Ten signs that you have body dysmorphia and 15 things to fix it

What's all the fuss about?

We are all guilty of spending a little too long in front of the mirror; whether that be in the bathroom, a compact you take with you everywhere or even a quick check in the car mirror/shop window.

Everyone has slight issues with their appearance and feeling constantly satisfied with ourselves isn't easy. We all have those days when our hair simply won't do what we tell it to or somehow overnight a huge spot (or two, or three) appears on your cheek right before an event. Many of us will occasionally feel dissatisfied, which is OK, and totally normal; however, these concerns don't cause extreme distress or completely occupy our thoughts. For some people however, said mirror checking becomes a habitual obsession with each and every perceived flaw, leading them to have regular, distressing thoughts. This behaviour, though mostly unheard of, yet relatively common, is called body dysmorphia.

Body dysmorphia can lead to distress, social anxiety, depression, self-harm and in some cases, suicide. Flaw checking can range in number and severity, be that worrying about the size or your nose, height, or aspiring to a certain body shape. Many of these hang ups are so small and barely noticeable (if at all) to others; however, sufferers of body dysmorphia don't see it that way. Many examine and obsess with their imperfections until it magnifies, leaving a distorted and unforgiving perception that others simply don't see. How we feel about our appearance is really important as it can affect our mood, our behaviour and our self-esteem.

Body dysmorphia comes as no surprise with the ever increasing rise in cultural and societal pressures to achieve physical perfection. Before the times of 'the selfie' you could only take a photograph with an old school film camera that your parents would always bring out on your birthday; with a single shot, a blinding flash and a quick hope for the best, the photo was taken and there was no going back (to anyone who has dared take a disposable to a festival – you can relate).

Nowadays, selfies have taken over; allowing us the freedom to take and view as many photos as we need until we find that perfect profile picture. However, we can also delete those that didn't quite make the cut, and use apps and features that 'help' us to edit and tweak any imperfections, which are all tools that makes us believe we're not good enough. It also raises the playing field, as more people use editing apps – it becomes a very distorted reality.

Body dysmorphia can range in severity, and for some, can seriously affect their lives. Below are some signs to spot if you or a friend/family member is suffering with this condition.

Ten signs that you may have body dysmorphia

⇨ You ask people if you look OK a lot: more often than not, it's because you're seeking validation from other people. It may feel good when they compliment you, but over a long period of time it's a really dangerous pattern of behaviour and will become increasingly compulsive.

⇨ You desperately want to meet a boyfriend or a girlfriend: sometimes people define their own value by their relationship status. Being single can be a stressful situation as it can validate the bad feelings that somebody may have about themselves – "nobody wants me" or "I'm not good enough". To be in a relationship is to temporarily feel validated or desired.

⇨ You check the mirror at every opportunity: checking the mirror can become a compulsive act and is a tell-tale sign that somebody isn't particularly feeling good about themselves. Body dysmorphia is a form of Obsessive Compulsive Disorder so it can be easy to become obsessed with attaining perfection.

⇨ You openly downplay your appearance to others: this tends to be because people have a fear of rejection. Think about it: your parents are pushing for you to do well in your exams. You came out and think you did OK but then tell your parents that the exam was really difficult. Why? Because you want to reduce their expectations of you so that it is less likely you'll feel rejected by them if you don't do well. It's a very clever tactic but it will not serve you well in the long term.

⇨ You're a selfie addict: we all like to take selfies now and again, but there's a line – and the very fact that you're reading this may suggest that you know you've crossed it. This is very similar to obsessively checking in the mirror in the sense that you're striving for perfection but also ties into the social validation. You want the perfect selfie to post online for the best possible reaction – right? The most likes. The most love heart eye emojis. It makes you feel good about yourself. But that's not good. You should never be looking externally for validation that you look OK.

⇨ You edit your photos or want plastic surgery: by definition, body dysmorphia means that you have a tainted view of yourself and see flaws that either don't exist or are barely noticeable. There's a difference between editing out a spot and changing your entire bone structure. If you're more inclined towards the latter, then it could suggest that there is a deeply rooted issue buried away in your self-esteem.

⇨ You get anxious in social situations sometimes: body dysmorphia can cause social anxiety – especially if you shy away from meeting new people or going on dates because you're worried that you don't look good enough. You're doing this because in your head, you believe that people won't want to talk to you or won't be interested in what you have to say because of your physical appearance. You then cleverly decide to avoid that situation to prevent your anticipations from becoming reality. We can almost completely guarantee that your anticipations will never happen and deep down, you know we're right.

⇨ You would never leave the house without make-up on: this could be one of the biggest tell-tale signs of body dysmorphia. You're scared of people seeing how you really look and fearful that they would reject you because your skin isn't flawless or because your hair isn't flowing. Make-up is great and can be used in positive ways, but there's a difference between enhancing your appearance and hiding behind it.

⇨ You're always dieting and picking at your body: body shape and size is a big hang up for a lot of people and it isn't surprising. Look at all the photoshopped pictures you've been shown since you were a kid in magazines and across the media. We all know they aren't realistic but they are there to make us feel like we're not good enough in order to sell us products. If you're worried about your body shape and size, you could very well be battling with body dysmorphia – especially if you factually have a healthy BMI.

⇨ You bitch about how other people look: the only reason people ever talk badly about how others look is to project how they feel about themselves onto other people. It's a way of basically saying "I feel bad about myself but wait... don't focus on me, look at her and the dress she's wearing." Once you understand that, you'll become very powerful.

15 tips on overcoming body dysmorphia

⇨ We are not medical practitioners and none of the advice below should be used to replace any advice you have been given medically. If you suspect you have body dysmorphia, we

would always recommend getting a formal diagnosis and support from your GP.

⇨ Remember that your mind is an incredibly powerful tool. What you think is what you will become. Actually, studies show that an affirming thought is 100 times more powerful than a negative one.

⇨ The Law of Attraction is a theory that suggests you attract things into your life simply by thinking about them. So if you spend all your time worrying about rejection, you're actually seeking it out and are more likely to experience it.

⇨ Go against your instinct and put yourself in social situations that make you feel uncomfortable. Acknowledging the fact that your mind is trying to protect you from rejection and going against those instincts can be incredibly powerful.

⇨ Limit the amount of times you're allowing yourself to look in the mirror or to check your reflection. It's a lot easier if you limit it gradually.

⇨ Be a rebel and stop editing your photos beyond using filters. However, it's important that you only do this when you feel comfortable doing it. You may

not be ready to yet and that's OK, but keep it in mind.

⇨ Acknowledge that there are things you dislike about yourself but don't focus on them any more. Nobody can make you feel bad about yourself, you do that.

⇨ Acknowledge that there are things you like about yourself and do focus on them. Even if you don't feel like there's anything, there is and as you become more comfortable in your own skin, this list will grow.

⇨ Understand that 98% of images you see of celebrities and models are edited and are not-representative. If you don't believe us, YouTube search "reverse Photoshop" or "models unedited" – it's okay that they have blemishes and stretch marks, because they are human.

⇨ Whenever you feel like saying something bad about how other people look, say something good about them too. Eventually work to stop saying bad things all together. Occasionally we all think negative things about others, that's normal but it isn't OK to vocalise them to others or use those opinions to make somebody feel bad about themselves to make yourself feel better.

⇨ Stop hanging around with people who make negative comments about how you look or make you feel pressured into looking a certain way. It's likely that they are going through the same thing too and trust us, you need to focus on you right now.

⇨ Understand that in 30 years, we guarantee you will look back at photos of yourself now and realise how fabulous you really looked.

⇨ Diversify your friendship circle and hang around with people you wouldn't otherwise hang around with. This will make you more familiar with different realities of appearances, body shapes and size.

⇨ Whenever you have a negative thought about yourself, acknowledge it and consciously decide to think of something positive. It sounds cliché but most of the time, you have 100% control over what you decide to think about – unless you are currently suffering a medical illness.

⇨ Be vocal and talk about it, but not too much. Don't overfocus on the negatives and talk more about how you're making changes and working on yourself. It is important not to keep it to yourself though. We'd suggest just talking about it to one or two people, no more, otherwise you'll find that you're talking about it too much.

⇨ Help somebody else overcome bad feelings they have about themselves and you could find that it also helps you overcome yours too.

⇨ The above information is reprinted with kind permission from Ditch The Label. Please visit www.ditchthelabel.org for further information.

When a negative body image becomes a mental health condition

Body image in the digital age

Recent research from YMCA revealed that 34% of teenage boys and 49% of teenage girls had been on a diet in an effort to change their body shape.[1] An issue which was previously seen as one primarily affecting girls has now been shown to be a problem for both genders.

The worrying state of young people's body confidence has been an ongoing issue in recent years, with several companies now beginning to address the situation.

Mattel, the company behind Barbie, has recently introduced a new range of the doll that comes in a range of shapes, heights, and hair and skin colours in an effort to broaden their representation of the female figure.

Having a positive body image is an important part of your overall sense of self-esteem. Having negative thoughts about how you look can impact on your entire life, and make it difficult to feel happy.

As a parent, you play a key role in building your child's confidence about their body, and making sure they have a healthy body image.

Sadly, a growing preoccupation with body image is a recurring theme of the digital age. Some claim that the popularity of selfies and posting photos onto social media has created a generation obsessed with their looks. Whether or not this is true, preoccupation with physical appearance is normal, especially during puberty.

But, when taking care over appearance tips over into the realms of obsession, it could be a sign that your child has BDD. Here, the charity BODY, explains more about this upsetting condition.

How does BDD differ from negative body image?

Body hang ups are common. You'd be hard pressed to find many people 100% happy with their body. But for people with body dysmorphic disorder (or BDD), a hang up can develop into an all-encompassing obsession which can make them deeply unhappy and put them at risk of other mental health problems, such as depression and self-harm.

BDD is a serious mental health condition characterised by a preoccupation with one or more flaws in appearance. These flaws are often minor or even non-existent, leading some to call BDD "imagined ugliness".

People with BDD become so hung up over their body image that it starts to have a negative effect on their entire life. This can range from continual extreme thoughts about corrective surgery to being completely housebound. They may avoid seeing friends or family, quit a job or start skipping school. People with BDD may also be at risk of self-destructive behaviour.

It isn't vanity

BDD is sometimes confused with vanity or attention-seeking behaviour, but it's important to remember that it's a serious mental health condition. People with BDD genuinely feel flawed or ugly and tend to be socially isolated, in part because they believe others will think they are vain. This often makes it harder to get help.

Sufferers of BDD usually focus on what they see as their flaws for up to eight hours a day, affecting one or all aspects of their life. People can concentrate their negative thoughts on any part of their body, but the most common areas to become preoccupied with are the skin, nose and hair.

People may focus on small features or on larger areas, like their muscles. For example, muscle dysmorphia sufferers believe they're small and weak even when they're large and muscular. This disorder is common in boys and men and has recently been reported on mainstream media, referred to as 'bigorexia'.

What are the symptoms of BDD?

The following behaviours are often warning signs of BDD. Some of these things can be warning signs for other issues, and some, like self-consciousness, are a normal part of growing up. But if your child

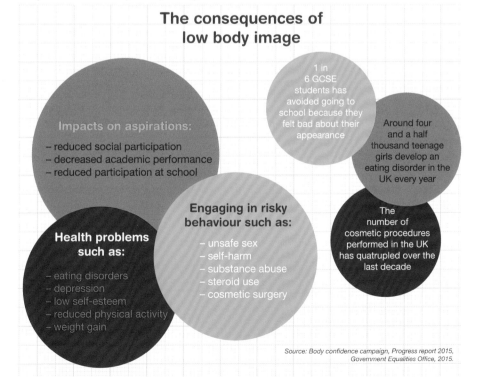

The consequences of low body image

Impacts on aspirations:
– reduced social participation
– decreased academic performance
– reduced participation at school

1 in 6 GCSE students has avoided going to school because they felt bad about their appearance

Around four and a half thousand teenage girls develop an eating disorder in the UK every year

Health problems such as:
– eating disorders
– depression
– low self-esteem
– reduced physical activity
– weight gain

Engaging in risky behaviour such as:
– unsafe sex
– self-harm
– substance abuse
– steroid use
– cosmetic surgery

The number of cosmetic procedures performed in the UK has quadrupled over the last decade

Source: Body confidence campaign, Progress report 2015, Government Equalities Office, 2015.

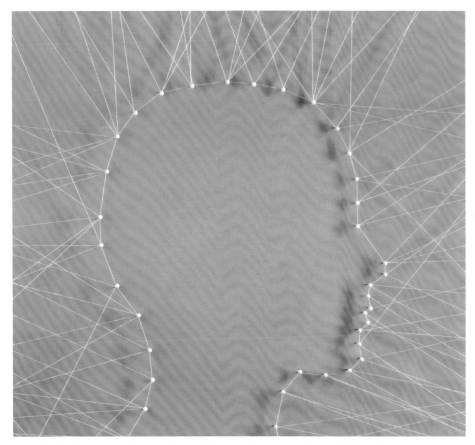

is displaying multiple signs, it's probably worth looking into more closely (see What to do if you think your child may have BDD, below).

⇨ Highly self-conscious.

⇨ Checking appearance in a mirror or reflective surface obsessively.

⇨ Distracted – struggling to concentrate on anything other than their appearance.

⇨ Increased self-isolation – not wanting to leave the house or go out and see friends.

⇨ Continually seeking reassurance about their appearance.

⇨ Picking at their skin to make it perfect.

⇨ Comparing themselves with other people, including celebrities in magazines or online.

⇨ Avoiding certain situations such as having their photograph taken, close-up interactions or being under bright lights/ surrounded by lots of mirrors.

⇨ Depressive thoughts and comments in relation to body image.

Research and findings on the condition

At the moment, there isn't enough information on BDD. Some research has shown, however, that it's more common in people with a family history of BDD, suggesting a possible genetic link. Similarly, a recent study showed that 80% of anorexics have family members who have also suffered from the disorder. BDD has also been linked to eating disorders. Unlike many eating disorders, though, BDD affects men and women equally.

What to do if you think your child may have BDD

Like many mental health conditions, BDD can sometimes come with a stigma attached, but people suffering from this isolating condition need help. The usual line of treatment is Cognitive Behavioural Therapy (CBT), but BODY, a charity focusing on helping those with BDD and other body image-related mental health problems, offers a variety of other therapies that can help too:

⇨ Support groups for loved ones and carers.

⇨ Self-help classes.

⇨ One-on-one therapy.

⇨ Creative expressive therapy workshops.

⇨ Occupational therapy.

⇨ Integrative psychotherapy.

⇨ The BODY Buddy national be-friending system.

If you think your child might have BDD, you should talk to them first. Tell them that you love them and are worried about them, and try to find out if there's something else that could be contributing to the issues you've noticed. It's important that you book an appointment with your GP. They'll be able to refer you onto a specialist who will be able to help your child.

Online resources to help people with BDD

⇨ BODY: http://www.bodycharity.co.uk/body-dysmorphic-disorder-bdd

⇨ Body Dysmorphic Disorder Foundation: http://bddfoundation.org/

⇨ OCD UK's section on BDD: http://www.ocduk.org/bdd

⇨ Books written by professionals on the condition:

  • http://bddfoundation.org/resources/books-by-professionals/

Reference

1. Read full YMCA report here: http://schoolsimprovement.net/wp-content/uploads/2016/02/World-of-Good-report-Central-YMCA.pdf

⇨ The above information is reprinted with kind permission from Parent Zone and CEOP. Please visit www.parentinfo.org for further information.

Boys and body image

Boys are affected by the media's depictions of unrealistic body types. Help them attain their own ideal – not someone else's.

By Caroline Knorr

Did you know?

⇨ Body image develops early in childhood.

⇨ Body image is influenced by family and culture.

⇨ Exposure to traditional media is a risk factor for developing body dissatisfaction.

Three facts about body image

⇨ The proportion of undressed males in advertising has been rising steadily since the 1980s.

⇨ 33–35% of boys aged six to eight indicate their ideal body is thinner than their current body.

⇨ The measurements of the male action figures young boys play with exceed even those of the biggest bodybuilders.

What's the issue?

The pursuit of a perfect body is no longer only a 'girl' thing. From padded Halloween superhero costumes that give five-year-olds six-pack abs to action movie stars with exaggerated physiques, representations of men in the media have become increasingly muscular and unrealistic. Boys are falling prey to the images of ideal bodies splashed across magazine covers; in video games, movies and music videos; and now on social media. Unlike their female counterparts, however, most boys aren't out to get skinny. They want to bulk up.

Big muscles are typically associated with good health. But what drives a young man to achieve that look can be far from healthy. Researchers have found a significant relationship between men's exposure to muscular-ideal media and negative self-image. With the advent of social media, online forums and blogs make it easy to seek and share information about diet and fitness. And some boys are going to extreme efforts to get a muscular, chiselled physique. Finally, frequent exposure to sexual material

Body image issues for boys

In a recent survey, 31% of UK men admitted to being dissatisfied with their bodies

Experts estimate **10% of male gym users** may be suffering from **muscle dysmorphia**. This leads them to underestimate their size and bulk and can lead to steroid abuse and depression

Guys are also increasingly reporting conditions such as anorexia and bulimia. In 2014, **300,000+ men** were admitted to hospital for **eating disorders** in the UK alone.

Source: Body image issues for boys, Channel 4, January 2016

can impact men's self-consciousness about their own appearance, as well as lead them to view women as sex objects.

Why body image matters for boys

Although research on boys lags behind that on girls, it's clear that negative self-image can affect boys' physical and mental health.

Boys are encouraged at an early age to think that being a man and being physically strong go hand in hand. As they grow older, the pressure to 'man up' can sometimes lead to crash diets, over-exercising, smoking, or even taking dangerous supplements. Exposure to highly sexualised material can impact men's self-esteem and relationships. And in a culture that discourages boys from talking about their feelings, it can be that much harder for parents to detect a son's body dissatisfaction.

What families can do

Make health a habit. If you take care of yourself, you'll help your kids appreciate all that bodies can do. By fostering a healthy lifestyle, you're helping your kids resist extreme dieting messages.

Look for alternative media. Avoid TV, movies and magazines that promote stereotypes and outdated gender roles. Seek out unconventional role models and talk about people from media and real life who have different body types and say why you find them

beautiful (for example, they're kind or wise).

Do a reality check. Point out that the sports celebrities they admire have teams of people helping them to work out, feeding them special meals and, in some cases, surgically altering them. The same holds true for 'hot' movie stars. One glance at the real men in their lives will drive home this point.

Keep an eye on your kid's social networks. Online, boys can feed their obsession in isolation. Bodybuilding and fitness forums can promote risky training and unattainable body ideals that boys may pursue without checking with a doctor or coach. Also, boys can expose themselves to constant criticism by posting photos of themselves.

Talk about 'real' girls. Highly sexualised media can distort boys' understanding of girls, relationships, and what the opposite sex looks like. Talk about how porn represents an extreme perspective that's not realistic.

⇨ The above information is reprinted with kind permission from Common Sense Media. Please visit www.commonsensemedia. org for further information.

© Common Sense Media 2016

France divides the fashion world by banning skinny models

French MPs pass a law making it illegal to employ unhealthily thin women or photoshop images without stating it clearly.

By Henry Samuel

France has sent shock waves through the global fashion industry by passing a surprise law making it a criminal offence to employ dangerously skinny women on the catwalk.

Under the new law, anyone running an agency found employing undernourished models below an as-yet undefined Body Mass Index, or BMI, risks a maximum six-month prison term and a €75,000 (£55,000) fine.

Magazines will also have to systematically indicate when a photograph of a model has been digitally 'touched up' to make her look skinnier or bulkier on pain of a €37,500 fine or up to 30 per cent of the sums spent on advertising.

The French fashion world reacted with anger, however, and described the measure as "a dangerous confusion between anorexia and the slimness of models" that will disadvantage Gallic agencies in what is a global industry.

French 'fashionistas' were already up in arms against another amendment passed on Thursday night that will make glorifying anorexia on the Internet a criminal offence. People who run so-called "pro-ana" or "thinspirational" websites risk a maximum year's imprisonment and a fine of €10,000 for "provoking people to excessive thinness by encouraging prolonged dietary restrictions that could expose them to a danger of death or directly impair their health". A host of websites or blogs claim to offer beauty tips to girls as young as 12, including starving themselves to create stick legs and a yawning "thigh gap".

Until Friday morning, it was assumed the second measure targeting modelling agencies would be dropped, as many MPs had pointed out that it would violate France's strict employment law on discrimination in job recruitment.

However, the National Assembly voted it through after health minister Marisol Touraine said the use of excessively thin models in fashion was "worrying" and that she backed the change.

Dr Olivier Véran, a Socialist MP and neurologist who tabled the amendment, said it was crucial to change mentalities in the fashion world about what is considered acceptable in terms of skinniness.

"The prospect of punishment will have a regulatory effect on the entire sector," he said, pointing out that Spain, Italy and Israel had already taken similar measures.

Spain bars models below a certain body mass index from featuring in the Madrid fashion shows; Italy insists on health certificates for models and Brazil is considering demands to ban underage, underweight models from its catwalks.

The World Health Organization considers people with a BMI below 18.5 to be underweight and at risk of being malnourished.

Arnaud Robinet with the opposition centre-right UMP party said the new law was "inapplicable and discriminatory" and would put the French fashion world at a disadvantage.

"Agencies will employ foreign models over French models," he claimed.

France's national model agency union Synam said a purely French approach would disadvantage the country's models.

"French model agencies are constantly in competition with their European counterparts. As a result, a European approach is essential," it said.

It also said the law "confuses anorexia with the slimness of models".

"When you look at criteria for anorexia, you can't just take BMI into consideration, but other criteria too, psychological but also whether models are losing hair or have teeth problems (due to undernourishment)."

The new law will ban any model whose BMI falls below a level fixed by France's Higher Health Authority.

But Isabelle Saint-Felix, secretary general of the union, insisted that some models, such as Ines de la Fressange, often dubbed the quintessential twiglike French model, were skinny by nature.

"She says herself that its part of her constitutional make-up, just like the rest of her family."

Dr Véran said a 2008 charter of good practice signed by the fashion industry had failed to change mentalities. During the parliamentary debate, he read out a letter from a top model explaining how agencies "congratulated girls who lose weight and recommend taking laxatives".

He cited one model who weighed "less than 45kg at 1.8m tall" whose friend died of a heart attack after coming off the catwalk due to "starvation".

There are an estimated 40,000 people in France suffering from anorexia, around 90 per cent of whom are adolescents.

3 April 2015

⇨ The above information is reprinted with kind permission from *The Telegraph*. Please visit www.telegraph.co.uk for further information.

Nine body positive social media campaigns that are changing how we perceive beauty both in and outside the fashion world

By Erin McKelle Fischer

It's no secret that the fashion industry has long been a culprit of body shame, with thin, white, photoshopped models having become the norm for almost 20 years, and the rest of us not in that demographic being pushed into the margins. But there are body positive social media campaigns combatting this narrow image of beauty – catering to the majority of women (and men) and redefining what 'beautiful' actually means.

And the good news is that things are actually starting to change. This year, plus-size models were seen taking over the runways of Fashion Week, diversity in fashion became more prevalent (although much work remains to be done), and the word 'fat' began to lose its status as a 'bad' or 'insulting' term. Yay, progress!

When we see a shift in cultural attitudes, the question everyone always asks is why. Why is it that sizeism is starting to become less socially acceptable and our relationships with body image a little less toxic? There's no surefire answer, of course, but we can certainly point to one obvious culprit: the Internet!

Social organisations online have become very popular in the last few years, as hordes of women have taken to platforms like Tumblr to talk about body image and reject our culture's body shame. Body positivity is trending and it's pretty awesome!

Relating this back to fashion, of course, here's a list of nine amazing social media campaigns that are changing the culture of fashion from fatphobic to all-body-loving.

1. #Fatkini

Since 2012, the #Fatkini movement has been going viral, featuring women of size taking selfies in their bathing suits. Where just a few years ago it might have been considered a rare occasion for a fat woman to be wearing a bathing suit, it's now being celebrated all over Twitter and Instagram.

The hashtag and movement was started by GabiFresh, a fashion blogger and body positivity advocate. She began the hashtag through a collaboration with xoJane, ultimately asking readers to submit photos of themselves wearing bathing suits. Soon after, the phrase went viral on social media. In fact, she generated so much buzz that she has now designed three collections of fatkinis for Swimsuits for All.

2. The Perfect Body

Last year, Victoria's Secret (VS) came out with a controversial campaign for their lingerie, entitled 'The Perfect Body'. The problematic nature was down to the women featured in the advertisements, who were all thin – ultimately not doing much as far as really encouraging women to love their bodies. In fact, thousands cried out asking the company to issue an apology and cease their campaign, and thankfully, VS changed the title to 'A Body For Every Body'.

But lingerie brands such as Curvy Kate Lingerie and Dear Kate decided to recreate the campaign using women of all shapes and sizes, representing real body diversity and love. Yay for body positivity!

3. #ImNoAngel

The hashtag and social media campaign #ImNoAngel by Lane Bryant is aiming to redefine what society considers to be sexy by

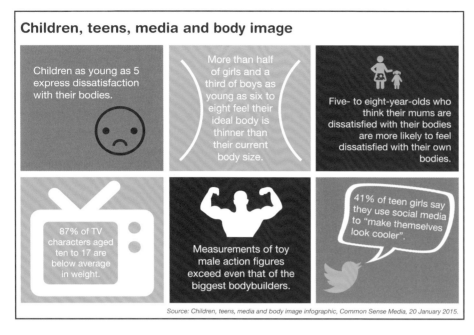

Children, teens, media and body image

Children as young as 5 express dissatisfaction with their bodies.

More than half of girls and a third of boys as young as six to eight feel their ideal body is thinner than their current body size.

Five- to eight-year-olds who think their mums are dissatisfied with their bodies are more likely to feel dissatisfied with their own bodies.

87% of TV characters aged ten to 17 are below average in weight.

Measurements of toy male action figures exceed even that of the biggest bodybuilders.

41% of teen girls say they use social media to "make themselves look cooler".

Source: Children, teens, media and body image infographic, Common Sense Media, 20 January 2015.

having women of all sizes submit photos of themselves using a "personal statement of confidence" with the hashtag. The campaign is being run primarily through the plus-size retailer's Tumblr page, which I think is also awesome, considering how much body positivity lives there! Although not everyone has considered the campaign to be a success (since the models featured in LB's initial ad were all generally of the same size), it is getting attention nonetheless, and definitely making waves – which I personally think always indicates a sign of success.

4. The Dove Campaign For Real Beauty

The Dove Campaign for Real Beauty is probably one of the most widely talked about social media campaigns that has ever been created, so how great is it that it lives at the intersection of body image and fashion? What I like the most about Dove's efforts is that they've been going on for over ten years and haven't just consisted of heart-warming commercials or social media posts – they've been doing real, groundbreaking research about body image! They've used their reports to create their campaigns on self-esteem and inner beauty, which have undoubtedly made an impact in our culture. Their latest effort is #speakbeautiful, in which they encourage women to engage in positive self-talk about their bodies.

5. Lose Hate, Not Weight

This social media campaign was spearheaded by fat activist Virgie Tovar, who has proclaimed that the philosophy behind the movement is to, "Seek to de-centre self-hatred and scarcity," or the "I am never good enough," mindset. Such a mindset is often the central motivator in people's lives, so this campaign aims to re-centre self-care and self-love, according to her personal website. Women have started to take photos of themselves on Instagram, reflecting this powerful message and taking proud ownership of their fat bodies.

6. Love Your Body

This has turned into more of a social movement than a specific campaign, but Love Your Body has overtaken the Internet and social media with its message to embrace your figure. Originally started by the National Organization for Women, they designated 14 October to be "Love Your Body Day" in order to take back to the oppressive beauty standards that society holds for women. It's now turned into an activist-fuelled movement with advertisements, videos, memes and more!

7. The What's Underneath Project

This project, started by Style Like U, is meant to redefine the ways in which we see other's bodies, going below the surface in a non-

objectifying, beautiful way. In fact, Bustle's own Marie Southard Ospina partook in this powerful campaign, which consists of videos of the subjects talking about themselves and their relationship with their bodies, as they slowly undress.

8. #LessIsMore

This hashtag was part of a petition created by eating disorder survivor Erin Treloar, in order to expose the fashion industry's heavy reliance on Photoshop to manufacture their impossibly perfect images and ask magazines to reduce their use of it. Treloar is also the founder and CEO of RAW Beauty Talks, an initiative to encourage girls to find confidence in their bodies. You can sign the petition if you want to talk back to fashion mags – it already has over 4,000 signatures!

9. #Fatshion

This sector of the body positivity movement has become a powerful force on social media websites like Tumblr and Instagram, where proud fat women have taken to the site to post their gorgeous selfies and outfits! The best part of this campaign is that it's grown organically and started a cultural conversation about body image and fashion – because obviously it is possible to love fashion and also be fat! I personally think this movement has led to the turning tides in plus-size fashion, with major retailers now getting on board selling fashionable, trendy clothes for people who happen to be over a size 12.

15 April 2015

⇨ The above information is reprinted with kind permission from Bustle. Please visit www.bustle.com for further information.

The A4 challenge is the 'horrifying' social media trend putting body image pressure on women

'We should be celebrating diversity.'

By Rachel Moss

Another day, another ridiculous social media campaign putting undue body image pressure on women.

The 'A4 Challenge' encourages women to see if their waists are smaller than an A4 sheet of paper.

'Successful' women then post a selfie with the paper onto social media, along with the hashtag #A4waist.

Needless to say the concept is laughable. The end image is entirely dependent on perspective and how far away you're holding the sheet of paper from your body.

The trend is reported to have started on Chinese social media site Weibo but unfortunately, it's now gaining global attention elsewhere.

Rivkie Baum, editor of plus size magazine *SLiNK*, thinks the trend is "horrifying".

"We already know that young girls spend far too much time on social media and that the influence of social media on their self-esteem is huge," she tells The Huffington Post UK.

"The A4 challenge does nothing to promote health and fitness but instead encourages young girls to evaluate themselves by their measurements and appearance.

"Being the size of an A4 piece of paper is not an accurate way to depict or assess health and perhaps it is time for social media to crack down on these types of irreverent campaigns that harm the young women that are so hooked on them."

Rebecca Field, head of communications at eating disorders charity Beat, agrees the trend could have a negative impact on vulnerable women.

"While social media cannot be the sole cause of an eating disorder, body image and low self-esteem are key factors in the development of eating disorders, and social and cultural pressures are strong in this area," she says.

"We should be celebrating diversity – women come in all shapes and sizes – not made to feel we don't 'shape up' by promoting such images. This is another example of how social media can encourage unhealthy messages."

Unfortunately this isn't the first time a body-shaming craze has emerged from China.

Last year the 'Belly Button Challenge' encouraged women to reach behind their own back and round their waist in an attempt to touch their belly button.

Then weeks later the 'Collarbone Challenge' encouraged participants to balance coins in their clavicle to test how 'skinny' they are.

Commenting on the latter movement, body image blogger Leyah Shanks told HuffPost UK: "I think this trend is very harmful. It's accentuating the idea that thinner is better and subsequently pushing down every other body type.

"Being able to do this is not what we should be basing our beauty and self-worth on.

"I'm not sure why these odd trends keep appearing. I wish that the power of social media would be used to spread body love instead of encouraging dangerous comparisons."

⇨ The above information is reprinted with kind permission from The Huffington Post UK. Please visit www.huffingtonpost.co.uk for further information.

© 2016 AOL (UK) Limited

'Daddy makeovers' and celeb confessions: cosmetic surgery procedures soar in Britain

A record number of over 51,000 Britons underwent cosmetic surgery in 2015, demonstrating the public's love affair with surgical enhancement is far from over, despite any previous 'blips' as the economy reshaped itself.

New data from the British Association of Aesthetic Plastic Surgeons (www.baaps.org.uk), the only organisation solely dedicated to safety and education in cosmetic surgery, and which represents the vast majority of NHS-trained consultant plastic surgeons in private practice, today reveal that the number of cosmetic ops last year grew 13% overall since 2014 – with ALL procedures seeing an increase in demand.

Surgeons say that with the new trend in A-list celebrities (such as Sharon Stone, Jamie Lee Curtis, Kelly Rowland, Jane Fonda and even *Modern Family*'s young starlet Ariel Winter) openly confessing to the odd nip or tuck, it's possible that patients are feeling encouraged by their positive admissions and attractive results. These new attitudes could be one of the drivers for increased acceptance and de-stigmatising of aesthetic enhancement, seven out of ten of the most popular procedures seeing a double-digit increase.

Women's cosmetic surgery rose 12.5% from 2014, and while breast augmentation continues to remain the most popular procedure for women (up 12% from 2014), reportedly the oversized 'glamour model' or artificial look once associated with implants has all but vanished, as surgeons note patients now opting for smaller sizes for a more natural, proportionate enhancement.

The Association also posits the theory that some of the most dramatic rises – face/neck lifts (up 16%) and liposuction (up 20%) – could be linked to the fact that despite the vast array of non-surgical treatments hyped for these areas in recent years, the public are realising they have limited effect when compared to traditional surgery.

Men, as well, underwent substantially more facial procedures, with face/necklifts climbing 14%, brow lifts (+15.5%), eyelid surgery (+15%), and rhinoplasty (+14%) all gaining huge popularity. Surgeons suggest that possibly, this may be nudged by the decline of last year's bushy-bearded 'hyper-masculine' (or 'lumbersexual') aesthetic common amongst hipsters. The trends could mean that as men ditched the facial hair and oversized checked shirts they may have uncovered previously-hidden double chins or 'dad bod' bellies fuelling an epic rise of 20% in male liposuction and a 13% jump in 'man boob' reductions.

Although men still account for just 9% of the total number of cosmetic surgery operations in the UK, their numbers have nearly doubled over the past decade (from 2,440 procedures in 2005 to 4,614 in 2015).

According to consultant plastic surgeon and former BAAPS President Rajiv Grover, who collated the audit data:

"The 2015 BAAPS audit has shown that demand for cosmetic surgery continues to increase following the quieter period in 2014 which mirrored the British economy. The double-digit rise in surgical procedures suggests that the public are choosing to spend on treatments with a proven track record such as facelifts and liposuction which remain as the gold standard for facial rejuvenation and body contouring. The plethora of new non-invasive methods for skin tightening and cellulite that are here today and gone tomorrow, often appear too good to be true and fail to make the cut.

"Perhaps the decline of the 'hyper-masculine' look fashionable last year which has given way to a sharper, more slimline shape has influenced men – and it certainly appears both genders seem encouraged by a new openness in glamorous celebrities admitting they have had 'a little surgical help' to enhance their looks. There is a danger however that this presents the image of cosmetic surgery as a commodity, so the public must always be warned that an operation is not something that can simply be returned to the shop if you don't like it."

Consultant plastic surgeon and BAAPS President Michael Cadier adds:

"There's no doubt that we are seeing an increase in demand for cosmetic surgery from both men and women. Whether this is inspired by celebrity culture and a recognition that the results of modern aesthetic procedures in the right hands can be subtle, natural-looking and attractive, what is most important is for patients to remember that surgery is on the whole life-changing and irreversible – far from a trivial 'status symbol' beauty treatment. The decision to undergo surgery must be well thought-out, with managed expectations, understanding the risks through fully informed consent and, most importantly, choosing the right specialist provider who is properly trained and accredited."

8 February 2016

⇨ The above information is reprinted with kind permission from The British Association of Aesthetic Plastic Surgeons. Please visit www.baaps.org.uk for further information.

© The British Association of Aesthetic Plastic Surgeons 2016

Smaller nose? Bigger boobs? Flatter stomach? There's an app for that

By Kate Harvey, Nuffield Council on Bioethics

Two weeks ago, beautiful Birmingham was home to a two-day workshop on the globalisation of beauty.

The workshop – organised by the network BeautyDemands – saw presentations from a wide range of contributors, but it was one issue in particular which led me to do a little further digging of my own.

A presentation by Professor Rosalind Gill focused on aesthetic entrepreneurship, which highlighted a body of work around beauty which she called, 'The quantified self'. This session explored, for example, how self-tracking and self-monitoring materialise in digital technologies, and change the way we may relate to ourselves.

The application of self-tracking and monitoring is clearly very relevant to health contexts: for example, smartphones are optimised to record how far we walk, how many calories we consume, or how well we sleep. However, over the past few years beauty apps available to mobile and tablet users have also suffused the market.

As a relative technophobe who mainly uses a smartphone to see if it's going to rain, and to find my way to the nearest bus stop (it's all glamour), beauty apps were very much off my radar. So I decided to find out more about them.

The Nuffield Council's current project on cosmetic procedures will focus primarily on invasive non-reconstructive cosmetic procedures (excluding temporary changes such as tanning or the application of make-up), so I restricted my searches to specific apps which focus on cosmetic procedures and surgeries. I gave myself just one hour to explore, fearing that weeks of my working life could quite easily be sucked into a chasm of curiosity.

One hour later, although significantly more enlightened on the range of cosmetic procedure apps, I was also the proud new owner of a couple of new frown lines.

The apps I found

According to Reuters, the first cosmetic surgery app (The Shafer Plastic Surgery App) was launched in 2009 by New York plastic surgeon Dr David Shafer. This app (no longer available through iTunes) enabled those considering cosmetic procedures to access over 1,000 FAQs on a range of procedures. Two years later, a press release from Medical Tourism NYC reported that Dr Shafer had developed another app to facilitate cosmetic procedure 'tourism' in New York City, or according to the press release, to "empower patients worldwide with access to information, travel and the ability to book appointments for the best aesthetic and surgical care available". This app thus clearly moves from answering questions to active facilitation of cosmetic procedures.

Similar facilitation can be found in other apps, which explicitly link to surgeons who could undertake procedures 'for real'. In a description of the app Lift/Tuck, for example, users are invited to "play around just for fun or send your results to Beverly Hills Celebrity Cosmetic Surgeon, Dr Garo Kassabian for a real life consultation". Another app, Breast Augmentation, developed by Dr Mark Glasgold, invites users to "download our app to easily request an appointment, to learn more about the procedures and techniques Dr Glasgold uses, and to view our before and after photos instantly. We have also included a treatment or recovery journal, where you can track your progress and attach photos easily to view your procedure outcome." Descriptions such as these perhaps indicate that cosmetic procedure apps are little more than thinly-veiled marketing tools.

Other apps attempt to distance themselves from 'real' procedures. For example, a disclaimer from the Plastic Surgery Simulator – an app which uses photo distortion, where facial features can be manipulated by dragging a finger across a touch-sensitive screen – includes a disclaimer: "There can be a huge difference between what can be achieved in the context of a real plastic surgery, and on this computer simulation tool. Only a real, certified surgeon will be able to assess what is realistically achievable. Always ask a certified plastic surgeon about possibilities, risks and financial cost of plastic surgery procedures."

Disclaimers such as these may, in part, be offered to avoid litigation should harm come to any of the apps' users. Other apps, however, take the possibility of future harm from cosmetic procedures as their sole purpose. Law firms may, for example, give people planning to have a procedure the opportunity to record every element of the process on an app, so that – should anything go wrong – they have a record which may support future negligence claims.

Just 'a bit of fun'?

Shortly after the release of the first Shafer App, iSurgeon was launched by Dr Michael Salzhauer (author of *My Beautiful Mommy,* a children's book focusing on a young girl whose mother undergoes abdominoplasty and rhinoplasty; as Zoe Williams wrote in *The Guardian* at the time, a book that might begin "Once upon a time, mommy had a tummy tuck…"). This app does not answer questions or facilitate, but rather invites users to play.

According to iSurgeon's website, the app "combines personal image modification with high tech gaming features", noting that it is "designed to allow users to simulate plastic surgery by easily modifying face and body features". This app is marketed as a game – indeed, its website address is isurgeongame.com – and Dr Salzhauer notes that the app "delivers on the promise of realistic photo alterations while also allowing users to partake in plastic surgery games playing the role of a surgeon". Closely associated with 'games' is 'fun', as is noted by the developers of Plastic Surgery Princess: "This app is for purposes of 'fun' only and is not for medical use or medical advice regarding aesthetic surgery or cosmetic surgery."

The 'gaming' aspect of some of the apps I found made me feel uneasy as I read various blurbs. For me, the invasiveness of cosmetic procedures and the potential vulnerabilities of those who might access those procedures, means that 'playing' with beauty ideals is a road which should be travelled down very cautiously, if at all. Indeed, more general caution in undergoing cosmetic procedures was urged earlier this week in a House of Commons adjournment debate when the Rt Hon. Ben Gummer (Parliamentary Under-Secretary of State for Health) observed that "people should think carefully about how they endorse cosmetic surgery. It is a serious intervention and if anyone seeks to glamorise something about which careful thought should be taken, people and the organisations using those endorsements should treat them with extreme care."

Concerns might also be raised in relation to the age of users for which apps are deemed suitable. For example, the link to the iSurgeon app through iTunes specifies that purchasers must be at least 17 years old to download the app; and ModYourBod is rated for those over the age of 12. In 2014, there was an outcry against an app which was rated as appropriate for those over the age of nine.

This app – 'Plastic Surgery & Plastic Doctor & Plastic Hospital Office for Barbie', which was marketed as a game – was withdrawn from iTunes following campaigns on social media. Its blurb, highlighted by a number of media outlets at the time (e.g. *The Independent*), depicted a cartoon image of an overweight girl, which was accompanied by the description that "[t]his unfortunate girl has so much extra weight that no diet can help her. In our clinic she can go through a surgery called liposuction that will make her slim and beautiful. We'll need to make small cuts on problem areas and suck out the extra fat. Will you operate her, doctor? [sic]" In a description offered by a piece published by *The Guardian*, users are then invited to tap on a surgical tool, then tap again on the body part on which that tool should be used, and "once the surgery is over there's an opportunity to play dress-up, with a choice of a few hairstyles, dresses and shoes". This app inarguably trivialised serious procedures, and did so by using language that could most kindly be described as 'highly insensitive'.

'Daring to dream'

So far, I've identified how apps may seek to promote or facilitate access to procedures; inform potential patients/consumers; or 'normalise' the use of surgery as a standard beauty procedure through gaming. One other purpose might be encapsulated in the phrase 'daring to dream'. Plastic Surgery: Thin and Tall, for example, entices users to consider: "have you ever dream [sic] about thigh gap and bikini bridge? Thin and tall application can make your dreams come true in a few seconds. Plastic Surgery: Thin and Tall is the best application to make you look handsome." Similarly, the ModYourBod app promises "your dream figure, at your fingertips" (this app also fits into the 'facilitation' category, as it enables users to request quotes for the procedure(s) they are interested in). The aspirational rhetoric of these apps again calls to question how they might affect potentially vulnerable audiences, especially given the low age threshold at which they are deemed suitable (Plastic Surgery: Thin and Tall, for example, is suitable for all ages).

Most of the applications I found during my one-hour search appear to focus on a female audience, so I quickly searched further specifically for apps that might be aimed at men. I came up with the a news item published in July 2014 by Marketwired which reported the "first ever male plastic surgery app" – called Manhattan Plastic Surgery for Men. This app is a hub for special offers and promotions for men considering undergoing cosmetic procedures, and provides access to relevant photos and "our private social media community". Again, this app is rated as suitable for people over the age of nine.

The only other app aimed at men which I found in my searches took me into the realm of 'giving' cosmetic procedures as gifts to woo women. According to a piece published by *Business Insider*, Carrot Dating (since banned from iTunes), enables men to "bribe their way to a date" (as an aside, the first line of the press release issued

by Carrot Dating is: "There's only one method of manipulation that has stood the test of time: bribery. It's a concept so simple that even animals understand – give a dog a bone, and it will obey. Give a woman a present, and she'll…") One of the bribes put forward as an option is the offer of plastic surgery to potential female partners.

At this point, I stopped searching, took a breath, made myself a strong cup of tea, and ate a custard cream.

One hour later...

Looking at the range of apps available was enlightening: in the course of an hour, I'm sure that I've only skimmed the surface of what's available. What I've identified in this blog therefore clearly isn't any better or worse than other apps I haven't written about – they're just simply those which I found first.

To complete my mini research exercise, I looked for evidence as to the effect of apps on people's motivation to actually undergo cosmetic procedures. I came up short. I found studies that report on the effect of reality TV, magazine consumption, and aspiring to film star looks. The proliferation of apps and their influence on those who access them, however, appears to be an area which hasn't been addressed empirically by researchers. Given that many people have smartphones and tablets clamped to their sides 24/7, this gap in evidence is something that needs to be addressed, and addressed soon.

26 October 2015

⇨ The above information was reprinted with kind permission from the Nuffield Council on Bioethics. Please visit www. nuffieldbioethics.org/project/ cosmetic-procedures/ for further information.

© Nuffield Council on Bioethics 2016

100 years of plastic surgery

Plastic surgery celebrates its 100th birthday this year. We examine how a medical procedure to treat soldiers in the trenches ended up being used to augment 50,000 Brazilians' buttocks.

By Harry Wallop

An astonishing 20 million plastic surgery procedures around the world were undertaken last year, according to new figures published this week. They included 50,000 pairs of buttocks being augmented in Brazil; 107,000 pairs of eyes being widened in South Korea – many of them to be made more 'western'; 1.35 million Americans having their breasts enlarged and 705 British men have their moobs removed. Don't ask about all the labiaplasty in Germany.

These statistics, published by the International Society of Aesthetic Plastic Surgery, show how far the concept of beauty has changed in the last generation, and hint at how, in many cultures, going to a cosmetic surgeon, rather than a cosmetics counter, is a guaranteed way to reduce the signs of ageing.

The figures would horrify Harold Gillies, who 100 years ago started a field of medicine forged in the bloody trenches of Flanders: modern plastic surgery.

The idea of grafting skin from one part of the body to another dates back centuries: 'plastic surgery' as a term was coined in the 1830s (from the Greek, plastikos – to be moulded), decades before 'plastic' became a word to describe man-made materials. But as Roger Green, archivist for the British Association of Plastic and Reconstructive Surgeons (BAPRAS), and himself a surgeon, says, the birth of modern plastic surgery can be dated to 1915.

Gillies was an ear, nose and throat surgeon, who volunteered to serve in the Red Cross in Belgium. "He saw new injuries that were pretty horrific," says Green. Many soldiers had their faces hideously disfigured by shrapnel as they poked their heads above the parapet.

Too severe to rectify with a skin graft, Gillies developed a technique called the tube pedicle, which involved cutting a strip of flesh from a healthy part of the body – usually the chest or forehead – but leaving one end still attached. The strip of skin was then 'swung' into the new area. The flap was folded in on itself, enclosing all the living tissue and blood supply, which prevented infection. The result looked bizarre, but it worked.

During the Battle of the Somme in 1917, Gillies treated 2,000 soldiers, mostly in this way.

During the Second World War, Archibald McIndoe, a pupil of Gillies, made further huge strides treating burnt airmen.

But it was not just McIndoe's technological advances, it was his whole approach, that were novel. "While Gillies's mantra was 'as long as I can fix someone, that's OK', McIndoe was more bothered about the psychology of patients," says Professor Tony Metcalfe, director of research at the Blond McIndoe Research Foundation. East Grinstead, where McIndoe's hospital was based, became "the town that didn't stare".

This right to a 'normal' life is something another pupil of Gillies has also pioneered, but for a very different type of patient. In Rio de Janeiro, Ivo Pitanguy, now 91, is called simply 'maestro' for his work in helping to popularise cosmetic surgery among not just the yacht-owning classes, but slum dwellers too. Last year over 1.3 million had work done in Brazil. "Aesthetic surgery brings the desired serenity to those that suffer by being betrayed by nature," he has said.

Pitanguy argues that cosmetic surgery heals ailments such as low self-esteem, an idea that has certainly gained traction in some cultures – in particular highly aspirational and fast-

growing economies like Brazil and South Korea, where an estimated 50 per cent of all women in their 20s have had work. Many Korean girls are given a facelift by their fathers as a graduation present – this is not anti-ageing, it is about transforming your features in order to improve your chances in life.

In some Seoul clinics, as part of their consultation, clients are asked to complete a questionnaire. One question asks what they intend to do after successful surgery. The options? "Get a lover", "find a job" or "upload a selfie without using Photoshop".

This sounds shocking but is not much different from the Hollywood stars of the 1920s, including Rudolph Valentino and Gloria Swanson, who had work done to their ears, noses and faces in an effort to land more roles, in an age when looks suddenly became magnified on the silver screen.

In Britain, cosmetic surgery is, mercifully, more regulated than in Korea, where it features on game shows. And after a decade of huge growth, the trend is for less invasive work – tweaks not tucks.

Indeed, breast enlargement surgery fell by 23 per cent last year in the UK, as many women were put off by the PIP scandal where many implants ruptured.

Also, the British attitude is different from South America or Asia.

"Patients don't want to look to as if they have been operated on. They want to look healthier, brighter, but not necessarily much younger," says Paul Harris, council member of the British Association of Aesthetic Plastic Surgeons, adding that for his patients the most popular breast size is "a full C".

Of course, for wealthy clients, the ultimate sin is to look 'done' like the infamous 'Bride of Wildenstein', the New Yorker Jocelyn Wildenstein, who spent a rumoured $4 million looking like a terrifying plastic cat. Or indeed Jennifer Grey, the *Dirty Dancing* actress, who bitterly regretted her rhinoplasty. "I went in the operating room a celebrity and came out anonymous," she has said of the surgery to straighten her distinctive nose.

People in the UK no longer want to change their appearance, as they might have done in the 1990s, but just "have more lustre", says Harris. "It's now all about being subtle."

Like the great majority of plastic surgeons in Britain, he works both for the NHS doing reconstructive work as well as undertaking cosmetic work for private patients.

And after nearly a century of cosmetic surgeons stealing ideas from reconstructive plastic surgery, the flow of knowledge is now going the other way. Fat transfer – pumping out fat from one area of the body, typically the stomach, and injecting it into the face is a case in point. Developed by cosmetic surgeons, it is now being used to help reconstruct breasts following cancer surgery.

Fat transfers are "alchemy", says Nigel Mercer, President of BAPRAS, but are still very risky. "The problem with fat is that it's got millions of stem cells, I mean millions." And with those stem cells comes a far higher chance of cancer developing once again.

100 years on, Gillies' pioneering work is also still being used to help people rebuild their lives. As well as pump up their buttocks.

10 July 2015

⇨ The above information is reprinted with kind permission from *The Telegraph*. Please visit www.telegraph.co.uk for further information.

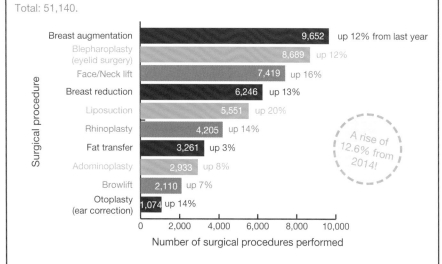

The top surgical procedures for men and women combined in 2015

Total: 51,140.

Surgical procedure	Number of surgical procedures performed	
Breast augmentation	9,652	up 12% from last year
Blepharoplasty (eyelid surgery)	8,689	up 12%
Face/Neck lift	7,419	up 16%
Breast reduction	6,246	up 13%
Liposuction	5,551	up 20%
Rhinoplasty	4,205	up 14%
Fat transfer	3,261	up 3%
Adominoplasty	2,933	up 8%
Browlift	2,110	up 7%
Otoplasty (ear correction)	1,074	up 14%

A rise of 12.6% from 2014!

Source: SUPER CUTS 'Daddy makeovers' and celeb confessions: cosmetic surgery procedures soar in Britain,
The British Association of Aesthetic Plastic Surgeons, 8 February 2016.

Lena Dunham bans media from photoshopping her: "If that means no more magazine covers, so be it"

By Rachel Moss, Lifestyle Writer at The Huffington Post UK

Lena Dunham has vowed she will no longer allow retouched images of herself to be used in the media after she "barely recognised herself" in a magazine recently.

Last week the *Girls* star accused Spanish magazine *Tentaciones* of Photoshopping an image of her on its front cover, but later issued an apology when the magazine said it did not retouch the image.

The publication claimed the image was approved by Dunham's agency, photographer and publicist and explained that the same photo was originally published by *Entertainment Weekly* in 2013, and had not been retouched by that publication either.

In an essay in her newsletter, *Lenny*, the actress says the incident has made up her mind about Photoshop once and for all.

"Something snapped when I saw that Spanish cover. Maybe it was the feeling of barely recognising myself and then being told it was 100% me but knowing it probably wasn't and studying the picture closely for clues," she writes.

"Maybe it was realising that was an image I had at some point seen, approved, and most likely loved. Maybe it was the fact that I no longer understand what my own thighs look like. But I knew that I was done."

In the essay, the 29-year-old goes on to admit that she enjoyed seeing her body retouched in the earlier stages of her career, but now she is making a public stand against such images.

"[I'm] done with allowing images that retouch and reconfigure my face and body to be released into the world. If that means no more fashion-magazine covers, so be it," she says.

She goes on to thank the likes of Kate Winslet, Jamie Lee Curtis and Zendaya for making her aware that "such a choice or statement was possible".

Dunham ends the letter by saying she wants to be honest with fans, but moreover, she wants to be honest with herself.

"This body is the only one I have. I love it for what it's given me. I hate it for what it's denied me," she says.

"And now, without further ado, I want to be able to pick my own thigh out of a lineup."

8 March 2016

⇨ The above information is reprinted with kind permission from The Huffington Post UK. Please visit www.huffingtonpost.co.uk for further information.

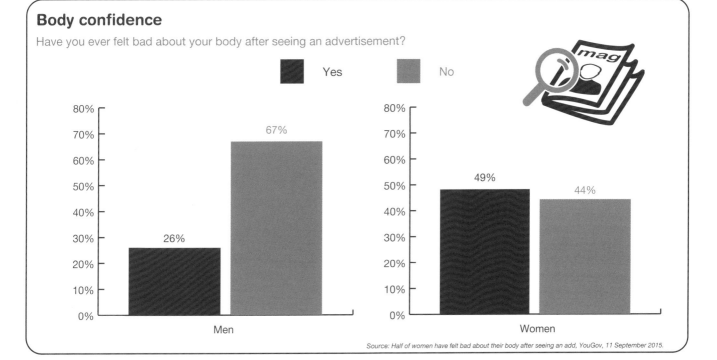

Body confidence

Have you ever felt bad about your body after seeing an advertisement?

■ Yes ■ No

Men: Yes 26%, No 67%

Women: Yes 49%, No 44%

Source: Half of women have felt bad about their body after seeing an add, YouGov, 11 September 2015.

The 'perfect body' is a lie. I believed it for a long time and let it shrink my life

As a child, Lindy West was told she was "off the charts". In this exclusive extract from her new book, Shrill, she explains how society's fixation on thinness warps women's lives – and why she would rather be 'fat' than 'big'.

By Lindy West

I've always been a great big person. In the months after I was born, the doctor was so alarmed by the circumference of my head that she insisted my parents bring me back, over and over, to be weighed and measured and held up for scrutiny next to the "normal" babies. My head was "off the charts", she said. Science literally had not produced a chart expansive enough to account for my monster dome. "Off the charts" became a West family joke over the years – I always deflected it, saying it was because of my giant brain – but I absorbed the message nonetheless. I was too big, from birth. Abnormally big. Medical-anomaly big. Unchartably big.

There were people-sized people, and then there was me. So, what do you do when you're too big, in a world where bigness is cast not only as aesthetically objectionable, but also as a moral failing? You fold yourself up like origami, you make yourself smaller in other ways, you take up less space with your personality, since you can't with your body. You diet. You starve, you run until you taste blood in your throat, you count out your almonds, you try to buy back your humanity with pounds of flesh.

I got good at being small early on – socially, if not physically. In public, until I was eight, I would speak only to my mother, and even then only in whispers, pressing my face into her leg. I retreated into fantasy novels, movies, computer games and, eventually, comedy – places where I could feel safe, assume any personality, fit into any space. I preferred tracing to drawing. Drawing was too bold an act of creation, too presumptuous.

My dad was friends with Bob Dorough, an old jazz guy who wrote all the songs for *Multiplication Rock*, an educational kids' show and *Schoolhouse Rock!*'s maths-themed sibling. He's that breezy, froggy voice on 'Three Is a Magic Number' – if you grew up in the US, you'd recognise it. "A man and a woman had a little baby, yes, they did. They had three-ee-ee in the family..." Bob signed a vinyl copy of *Multiplication Rock* for me when I was two or three years old. "Dear Lindy," it said, "get big!" I hid that record as a teenager, afraid that people would see the inscription and think: "She took that a little too seriously."

I dislike "big" as a euphemism, maybe because it's the one chosen most often by people who mean well, who love me and are trying to be gentle with my feelings. I don't want the people who love me to avoid the reality of my body. I don't want them to feel uncomfortable with its size and shape, to tacitly endorse the idea that fat is shameful, to pretend I'm something I'm not out of deference to a system that hates me. I don't want to be gentled, like I'm something wild and alarming. (If I'm going to be wild and alarming, I'll do it on my terms.) I don't want them to think I need a euphemism at all.

"Big" is a word we use to cajole a child: "Be a big girl!" "Act like the big kids!" Having it applied to you as an adult is a cloaked reminder of what people really think, of the way we infantilise and desexualise fat people. Fat people are helpless babies enslaved by their most capricious cravings. Fat people don't know what's best for them. Fat people need to be guided and

Social body pressure

Do you think that society puts too much or too little pressure on men/women to be fit and attractive?

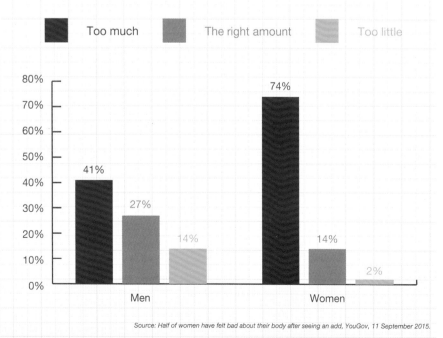

Source: Half of women have felt bad about their body after seeing an add, YouGov, 11 September 2015.

scolded like children. Having that awkward, babyish word dragging on you every day of your life, from childhood into maturity, well, maybe it's no wonder I prefer hot chocolate to whisky and substitute Harry Potter audiobooks for therapy.

Every cell in my body would rather be "fat" than "big". Grown-ups speak the truth.

Over time, the knowledge that I was too big made my life smaller and smaller. I insisted that shoes and accessories were just "my thing", because my friends didn't realise I couldn't shop for clothes at regular shops and I was too mortified to explain it to them. I backed out of dinner plans if I remembered the restaurant had particularly narrow aisles or rickety chairs. I ordered salad even if everyone else was having fish and chips. I pretended to hate skiing because my giant men's ski pants made me look like a chimney and I was terrified my bulk would tip me off the chairlift. I stayed home as my friends went hiking, biking, sailing, climbing, diving, exploring – I was sure I couldn't keep up, and what if we got into a scrape? They couldn't boost me up a cliff or lower me down an embankment or squeeze me through a tight fissure or hoist me from the hot jaws of a bear. I never revealed a single crush, convinced that the idea of my disgusting body as a sexual being would send people – even people who loved me – into fits of projectile vomiting (or worse, pity). I didn't go swimming for a decade.

As I imperceptibly rounded the corner into adulthood – 14, 15, 16, 17 – I watched my friends elongate and arch into these effortless, exquisite things. I waited. I remained a stump. I wasn't jealous, exactly; I loved them, but I felt cheated.

We each get just a few years to be perfect. To be young and smooth and decorative and collectible. That's what I'd been sold. I was missing my window, I could feel it pulling at my navel (my obsessively hidden, hated navel), and I

scrabbled, desperate and frantic. Deep down, in my honest places, I knew it was already gone – I had stretch marks and cellulite long before 20 – but they tell you that, if you hate yourself hard enough, you can grab a tail feather or two of perfection. Chasing perfection was your duty and your birthright, as a woman, and I would never know what it was like – this thing, this most important thing for girls.

I missed it. I failed. I wasn't a woman. You only get one life. I missed it.

Society's monomaniacal fixation on female thinness isn't a distant abstraction, something to be pulled apart by academics in women's studies classrooms or leveraged for traffic in shallow 'body-positive' listicles ('Check Out These 11 Fat Chicks [...] No 7 Is Almost Like a Regular Woman!'). It is a constant, pervasive taint that warps every woman's life. And, by extension, it is in the amniotic fluid of every major cultural shift.

Women matter. Women are half of us. When you raise women to believe that we are insignificant, that we are broken, that we are sick, that the only cure is starvation

and restraint and smallness; when you pit women against one another, keep us shackled by shame and hunger, obsessing over our flaws, rather than our power and potential; when you leverage all of that to sap our money and our time – that moves the rudder of the world. It steers humanity toward conservatism and walls and the narrow interests of men, and it keeps us adrift in waters where women's safety and humanity are secondary to men's pleasure and convenience.

I watched my friends become slender and beautiful, I watched them get picked and wear J Crew and step into small boats without fear, but I also watched them starve and harm themselves, get lost and sink. They were picked by bad people, people who hurt them on purpose, eroded their confidence and kept them trapped in an endless chase. The real scam is that being bones isn't enough, either. The game is rigged. There is no perfection.

I listened to Howard Stern every morning in college on his eponymous 90s' radio show. *The Howard Stern Show* was

magnificent entertainment. It felt like a family. Except that, for female listeners, membership in that family came at a price. Stern would do this thing (the thing, I think, that most non-listeners associate with the show) where hot chicks would turn up at the studio and he would look them over like a horse vet – running his hands over their withers and flanks, inspecting their bite and the sway of their back, honking their massive horse jugs – and tell them, in intricate detail, what was wrong with their bodies. There was literally always something. If they were eight stone, they could stand to be seven. If they were six, gross. ("Why did you do that to your body, sweetie?") If they were a C cup, they'd be hotter as a DD. They should stop working out so much – those legs are too muscular. Their 29in waist was subpar – come back when it's a 26.

Then there was me: 16 stone, 40in waist, no idea what bra size, because I'd never bothered to buy a nice one, because who would see it? Frumpy, miserable, cylindrical. The distance between my failure of a body and perfection stretched away beyond the horizon.

According to Stern, even girls who were there weren't there.

If you want to be a part of this community that you love, I realised – this family that keeps you sane in a shitty, boring world, this million-dollar enterprise that you fund with your consumer clout, just as much as male listeners – you have to participate, with a smile, in your own disintegration. You have to swallow, every day, that you are a secondary being whose worth is measured by an arbitrary, impossible standard administered by men.

When I was 22 and all I wanted was to blend in, that rejection was crushing and hopeless and lonely. Years later, when I was finally ready to stand out, the realisation that the mainstream didn't want me was freeing and galvanising. It gave me something to fight for. It taught me that women are an army.

When I look at photographs of my 22-year-old self, so convinced of her own defectiveness, I see a perfectly normal girl and I think about aliens. If an alien – a gaseous orb or a polyamorous cat person or whatever – came to

Earth, it wouldn't even be able to tell the difference between me and Angelina Jolie, let alone rank us by hotness. It'd be like: "Uh, yeah, so those ones have the under-the-face fat sacks, and the other kind has that dangly pants nose. F***, these things are gross. I can't wait to get back to the omnidirectional orgy gardens of Vlaxnoid."

The 'perfect body' is a lie. I believed in it for a long time, and I let it shape my life, and shrink it – my real life, populated by my real body. Don't let fiction tell you what to do. In the omnidirectional orgy gardens of Vlaxnoid, no one cares about your arm flab.

8 May 2016

Self-esteem is how you feel about yourself

People with high self-esteem:

⇨ Feel good about themselves, most of the time.

⇨ Respect themselves.

⇨ Take responsibility for their feelings, thoughts and actions.

⇨ Tend to think of mistakes or problems as chance to grow and change.

⇨ Have a positive attitude.

⇨ Show good judgment.

⇨ Demonstrate good problem-solving skills.

⇨ Maintain healthy, close relationships.

⇨ Have confidence in new situations.

⇨ Try new things with courage and zest.

⇨ Are trustworthy.

⇨ Are self-motivated.

⇨ Are open to feedback.

⇨ Aren't afraid to seek goals that may be challenging.

People with low self-esteem:

⇨ Don't believe in themselves.

⇨ Often seek approval from others.

⇨ Participate in things at others' requests.

⇨ View mistakes or problems as personal failures and internalise these failures as a reflection of their selves.

⇨ Have a negative attitude.

⇨ Have poor judgment.

⇨ Possess poor problem-solving skills.

⇨ Have unhappy relationships.

⇨ Are nervous in new situations.

⇨ Don't stand up for themselves, their values or beliefs.

⇨ Let other people take advantage of them.

⇨ Have difficulty saying "no".

⇨ Tend to be self-critical of their body, behaviour and life.

Low self-esteem can lead to:

⇨ Excessive worry

⇨ Depression

⇨ Alcohol, tobacco, or other drug use/abuse

⇨ Eating concerns

⇨ Suicide

⇨ Poor body image

⇨ Unhealthy relationships

⇨ Making unhealthy sexual health decisions

⇨ Anger and aggressive behaviour.

Who and what influences our self-esteem?

⇨ Family members

⇨ Friends

⇨ Teachers, coaches, caregivers

⇨ The media

⇨ Strangers

⇨ Experiences.

From the moment of birth, our self-esteem begins to take shape by what others think about us and how we are treated. Family members and caregivers are powerful influences on shaping our early self-esteem. As children, we didn't have the ability to critique messages or form our own opinions of ourselves. We saw ourselves through the eyes of others.

If we were treated positively, valued and nurtured as children, chances are we have high self-esteem.

If we were neglected, given negative messages, such as being told we were "stupid" or "bad", chances are we have lower self-esteem.

Though childhood provides the foundation for our self-esteem, it is hoped as we get older and gain a sense of self that external influences have less impact on our self-esteem.

How can I change my self-esteem?

⇨ Let go of negative messages we received as children

⇨ Notice and stop negative self-talk

⇨ Don't call yourself, "dumb", "fat", "ugly", "weak", "a failure", "an idiot"

⇨ Notice the things you like about yourself

⇨ You can work to change the things you don't like about yourself

⇨ There is no such thing as being perfect, so let go of that idea

⇨ Take responsibility for your actions

⇨ Think openly and critically about feedback from others

⇨ Don't base your self-worth on messages from the media

⇨ Raising self-esteem takes time, patience and hard work. It's not easy, but it can be done!

⇨ Develop a sense of who you are as an individual

⇨ Surround yourself with people who care and support you for who you are.

⇨ The above information is reprinted with kind permission from the University of New Hampshire Health Services. Please visit unh.edu for further information.

© University of New Hampshire Health Services 2016

Consequences of low self-esteem

How is low self-esteem related to mental health?

Low self-esteem is not a recognised mental health problem, but self-esteem and mental health are closely related.

Low self-esteem can lead to mental health problems

⇨ Negative thinking patterns associated with low self-esteem, such as assuming you will fail at things you do, can develop over time and lead to mental health problems such as depression or anxiety.

⇨ Low self-esteem can make it hard to try new things or complete tasks, such as starting a new hobby or completing a job application. This can stop you from living your life the way you want, and lead to frustration and depression over time.

⇨ If you find certain situations difficult because of low self-esteem, you may start to avoid them and become increasingly socially isolated. This can cause feelings of anxiety and depression that can develop into mental health problems over time.

⇨ Low self-esteem can cause people to develop unhelpful behaviours as a way of coping, such as forming damaging relationships, taking drugs or drinking too much. This often causes problems in the long term and makes life more difficult, which can then lead to mental health problems.

Mental health problems can cause low self-esteem

Some mental health problems, such as eating problems, depression and social phobia, involve developing negative thinking patterns about yourself.

⇨ A mental health problem can make it hard to do day-to-day tasks, such as using public transport or maintaining a paid job. This can have a negative impact on the way you see yourself.

⇨ A mental health problem could cause you to withdraw from social contact, if you are worried how other people may see you. This can lead to feelings of isolation and loneliness, which can then cause low self-esteem.

⇨ Stigma and discrimination about mental health problems could mean you develop a negative opinion about yourself.

Cycle of low self-esteem and mental health problems

Low self-esteem and mental health problems can reinforce each other, creating an unhelpful cycle.

What can I do to build my self-esteem?

In order to increase your self-esteem, you need to challenge and change the negative beliefs you have about yourself. This might feel like an impossible task, but there are a lot of different techniques you can try to help you.

Do something you enjoy

Doing something that you enjoy, and that you are good at, can help build your confidence and increase your self-esteem. This could be anything from paid work, volunteering, caring or a hobby.

Work

Work can provide identity, friendship, a steady routine and a salary. Some people thrive in a busy environment and enjoy working to ambitious targets. Other people see their job as a means to an end or work in unpaid, volunteering roles. Whatever you do, it is important that you feel confident and supported in your role, and that the balance between your work and your home-life feels right for you. (See Mind's booklet *How to be mentally healthy at work* for information about looking after your mental health while in paid employment.)

Hobbies

This could be anything from learning a language, to singing, to a painting class. Think about where you feel you have some natural ability, or things that you have always wanted to try. Try to find activities that will not challenge you too much to begin with so that you can feel you have achieved something and have a chance to build your confidence. The Internet, your library and adult education colleges should have details of local clubs and classes that you might want to go along to.

Try to build positive relationships

Try to associate with people who will not criticise you, and who you feel able to talk to about your feelings. If you spend time around positive and supportive people, you are more likely to have a better self-image and feel more confident.

In return, if you are caring and supportive to other people, you are more likely to get a positive response from them. This will help you feel better about yourself and how other people perceive you.

If you have low self-esteem, there might be people close to you who encourage the negative beliefs and opinions that you hold. It is important to identify these people and take action to stop them from doing this, perhaps by becoming more assertive (see 'Learn to be assertive' below) or by limiting how much you see them.

Learn to be assertive

Being assertive means you value yourself and others, and can communicate with mutual respect. It will help you to set clear boundaries. The following things will help you act in a more assertive way:

⇨ Pay attention to your body language as well as to the words you say – try to be open and confident.

⇨ Try to express your feelings if you have been upset – wait until you feel calm and explain clearly how you feel.

⇨ Say "no" to unreasonable requests.

⇨ Tell people if you need more time or support with tasks that you find challenging.

⇨ Try to speak in the first person where possible – e.g. "When you speak to me like that, I feel…". This allows you to explain what you want to happen without appearing aggressive or scared.

⇨ Assertiveness can be a difficult skill to learn, and you may need to practise by talking in front of a mirror or with a friend. Many adult education institutions, such as colleges or universities, also offer assertiveness classes. There are also several self-help books with practical exercises and tips available to buy or use online.

Look after your physical health

Looking after your physical health can help you feel happier and healthier, and improve your self-image.

Physical activity

Physical activity helps improve people's sense of wellbeing and image of themselves. Exercise releases endorphins – 'feel-good' hormones that can help improve your mood, particularly if you do it outside. (See Mind tips for better mental health: physical activity for ideas on how to get active.)

Sleep

Lack of sleep can cause negative feelings to be exaggerated and means you can feel less confident, so it's important to make sure you get enough sleep. (See Mind's booklet *How to cope with sleep problems* for help establishing a good sleep routine.)

Diet

Eating a well-balanced diet at regular meal-times with plenty of water and vegetables will help you to feel healthier and happier. Stopping or reducing your alcohol intake, and avoiding tobacco and recreational drugs can also help improve your general wellbeing.

Set yourself a challenge

If you set yourself goals and work towards achieving them, you will feel satisfied and proud of yourself when you achieve your goal, and feel more positive about yourself as a result.

Make sure the challenge you set yourself is one that you can realistically achieve. It doesn't have to be anything particularly large but should have meaning for you. For example, you might decide you are going to write a letter to your local paper or start going to a regular exercise class.

Learn to identify and challenge negative beliefs

If you are going to improve your self-esteem, it may also help to understand more about your negative beliefs about yourself and where they came from.

This could be a painful process, so it's important to take your time, and perhaps ask a friend or partner to support you. If you are feeling very distressed, it might be better to seek professional help from a therapist to help you do this.

It might be helpful to write down notes, and questions such as these could help to structure your thoughts:

⇨ What do you feel are your weaknesses or failings?

⇨ What negative things do you think other people think about you?

⇨ If you could sum yourself up, what word would you use – "I am…"?

⇨ When did you start feeling like this?

⇨ Can you identify an experience or event that might have caused this feeling?

⇨ Do you find you have certain negative thoughts on a regular basis?

It might also be helpful to keep a thought diary or record over a period of several weeks. Write down details of situations, how you felt and what you think the underlying belief was. For example:

Situation	Reaction	Underlying belief
Asked to deliver a presentation at work	Felt very anxious, but told boss it was fine	No-one will want to listen to me because I am not engaging
I was invited to a party	I lied and said I had something else to do	I can't say anything interesting and I'll look stupid dressed up
I saw a job that I liked in the paper	I got angry and tore it up	I'm not clever enough for that sort of work or someone would have offered me a job like that already

As you identify what your core beliefs about yourself are, and where they come from, you can begin to challenge and change them. One way you can do this is to write down evidence to challenge each belief and begin to explore other explanations of a situation.

For example, if you think that no one likes you, you can start to record situations that show a different pattern:

⇨ My mum called me on my birthday.

⇨ My brother didn't answer my call, but then later told me he had been really busy at work – it wasn't personal.

⇨ I have been asked to go to a friend's wedding next summer.

⇨ I had a really nice conversation with my colleague over our coffee break.

These might feel like small examples, but as your list gets longer over time you can look back at it and challenge the negative

opinions that you have been holding on to.

You could make a list of negative thoughts with the evidence against them, in two columns:

Negative thought | Evidence against it

Focus on positive things

If you have low self-esteem, it can take practice to get used to thinking more positively about yourself. One way you can do this is by making a list of several things that you like about yourself.

You might include:

⇨ things about your personality

⇨ things about the way that you look

⇨ things that you do

⇨ skills you have developed.

Take your time and aim for 50 different things, even if this takes several weeks. Keep this list and look at a different part of it each day. If you are feeling down or worried about an event that is coming up, such as a job interview, you can use it to remind you of the good things about yourself.

If you struggle to come up with a list of good things, you could ask your partner or a trusted friend to help you begin. This may also help you to see how others may have a higher opinion of you than you do yourself.

Another technique is to write down at least three things that went well or that you have achieved that day before you

go to sleep. Some people also find it helpful to keep objects, such as photos or letters that make them feel good about themselves.

You might like to make a list of positive things about you.

Try mindfulness techniques

Mindfulness is a way of paying attention to the present moment, using techniques like meditation, breathing and yoga. It has been shown to help people become more aware of their thoughts and feelings, so that instead of being overwhelmed by them, it is easier to manage them. The Be Mindful website has more information and details of local classes around the UK. There are also many mindfulness self-help books and CDs available.

Self-help resources

Ten tips to increase your self-esteem:

1. Do activities that you enjoy.

2. Spend time with positive, supportive people.

3. Be helpful and considerate to others.

4. Try not to compare yourself to other people.

5. Try to do regular exercise, eat healthily and get enough sleep.

6. Be assertive – don't let people treat you with a lack of respect.

7. Use self-help books and websites to develop helpful skills, like assertiveness or mindfulness.

8. Learn to challenge your negative beliefs.

9. Acknowledge your positive qualities and things you are good at.

10. Get into the habit of thinking and saying positive things about yourself.

⇨ The above information is reprinted with kind permission from Mind. Please visit www.mind.org.uk for further information.

When do children show evidence of self-esteem? Earlier than you might think

An article from The Conversation.

THE CONVERSATION

By Dario Cvencek, Research Scientist, University of Washington, Andrew N. Meltzoff, Professor and Co-Director, Institute for Learning & Brain Sciences, University of Washington and Anthony G. Greenwald Professor of Psychology, University of Washington

A YouTube clip called 'Jessica's Daily Affirmation' recently went viral. The clip shows a four-year-old Jessica standing in front of the bathroom mirror saying what makes her happy about herself.

Many youngsters, like Jessica, seem to exude positive feelings about their abilities – they happily report that they are good at running, jumping, drawing, maths or music.

However, the belief in being good at certain concrete skills could be different from a more general sense of self-worth or what scientists call "positive self-esteem" For example, at early ages, children can report "I'm good at running" or "I'm good with letters". But preschoolers might not be able to answer questions about their overall sense of self-worth.

So, when do kids develop a sense of self-esteem and how can we measure it?

Our research has developed new ways to study what kids think about themselves. Parents, make a note: our results show that most kids develop a sense of self-esteem – feeling good or bad about oneself – as early as age five, before they even enter kindergarten.

Measuring self-esteem in young children

Measuring children's self-esteem can be challenging because it seems to require a certain level of introspection and verbal abilities. We found a way of getting around this by measuring children's deeper and more implicit sense of self-esteem, something that did not require answering verbal questions.

For example, in adults, self-esteem is often measured by asking people to rate their agreement with statements such as, "I feel that I am a person of worth, at least on an equal plane with others," or "I take a positive attitude toward myself."

But preschoolers have difficulty answering such verbal questions. Cognitive and verbal skills required for such answers do not develop before age eight.

So, rather than relying on asking children verbal questions, we developed a new tool called the 'Preschool Implicit Association Test' (the PSIAT) to measure children's implicit self-esteem. The value of this measure was that it did not require children to verbally describe how they felt about themselves.

Here's how we did it.

We gave two sets of small coloured flags, each set symbolizing 'me' and 'not me', to 234 children.

These children then were asked to respond to a series of 'good' (fun, happy and nice) and 'bad' (mad, mean and yucky) words from a loudspeaker by pressing buttons. This procedure measured how closely the children associated the 'good' words with the 'me' flags.

This procedure is a variation of the adult Implicit Association Test, a social psychology measure widely used to reveal hidden biases in adults about race, religion, self and other topics by asking participants to quickly categorise words from different categories.

We found that more than 90 per cent of five-year-old preschoolers linked themselves with the 'good' words, which indicated positive self-esteem. It also showed us that most kids develop a measurable sense of self-esteem by age five.

Our test provides researchers with a reliable way of examining the earliest glimpses of how preschoolers develop a sense of their self-worth.

People with high self-esteem more resilient

So, why is self-esteem important for children?

A healthy self-esteem can provide an emotional buffer to setbacks and enable children to develop resilience toward failures. In adults, self-esteem has been shown to predict an individual's reactions to success and failure. People who have high self-esteem persist more after experiencing a setback than do people who have low self-esteem.

In young children, such a relationship between resilience and self-esteem may be especially important to early learning and education.

For example, few first graders consistently score 100 per cent on all tests, and few preschoolers are as skilled as their older siblings. We believe that such micro-setbacks can be buffered by positive self-esteem.

Because self-esteem tends to remain relatively stable across one's lifespan, its early establishment could potentially provide a lifelong emotional buffer in the face of everyday failures and challenges.

The importance of self-esteem

How do children develop their sense of self-esteem?

Young kids care a lot about others 'like me', and this may even start in infancy. We also know from other research that infants and toddlers can judge the extent to which others are like them along several dimensions.

This lays the foundation for developing social relationships and a sense of belonging. These feelings, combined with warm and consistent care, help children develop feelings of attachment to their parents, which may further pave the way for the development of positive self-esteem. We found the first five years to be critical in laying the foundation for this social-emotional development.

Positive self-esteem can help in other ways as well.

For preschoolers, it is important to feel that they are part of a group. In this way they can navigate the social world more easily. Children, just like adults, tend to prefer those groups to which they belong.

Scientists call this an in-group preference. In-groups in adults can be based on race, nationality, religion, etc. In children, we found a strong in-group preference based on gender, and it was linked to self-esteem.

This shows that self-esteem is systematically related to other fundamental aspects of one's personality very early in development. We believe that self-esteem is one of the mental tools children use to create a sense of identity and belonging with social groups. In other words, at an early age, children mirror adult patterns of psychological organisation. This is something they bring to kindergarten with them and don't learn in school.

Giving kids a good start in life may be one of the most important gifts that parents can provide to their child: children who feel loved by others will likely internalise this love to love themselves.

Jessica from the YouTube video is but one compelling reminder of just how inspiring a young child's positive self-view can be. And it is the foundation for so much more.

22 January 2016

⇨ The above information is reprinted with kind permission from *The Conversation*. Please visit www.theconversation.com for further information.

Raising low self-esteem

We all have times when we lack confidence and don't feel good about ourselves.

But when low self-esteem becomes a long-term problem, it can have a harmful effect on our mental health and our lives.

Self-esteem is the opinion we have of ourselves. When we have healthy self-esteem, we tend to feel positive about ourselves and about life in general. It makes us able to deal with life's ups and downs better.

When our self-esteem is low, we tend to see ourselves and our life in a more negative and critical light. We also feel less able to take on the challenges life throws at us.

What causes low self-esteem?

Low self-esteem often begins in childhood. Teachers, friends, siblings, parents, and even the media give us lots of messages – both positive and negative. But for some reason, the message that you are not good enough sticks.

You may have found it difficult to live up to other people's expectations of you, or to your own expectations.

Stress and difficult life events, such as serious illness or a bereavement, can have a negative effect on self-esteem. Personality can also play a part. Some of us are simply more prone to negative thinking, while others set impossibly high standards for themselves.

How does low self-esteem affect us?

The problem with thinking we're no good is that we start to behave as if it's true. "Low self-esteem often changes people's behaviour in ways that act to confirm the person isn't able to do things or isn't very good," says Chris Williams, Professor of Psychosocial Psychiatry at the University of Glasgow.

If you have low self-esteem or confidence, you may hide yourself away from social situations, stop trying new things and avoid things you find challenging.

"In the short term, avoiding challenging and difficult situations makes you feel a lot safer," says Professor Williams. "In the longer term, this avoidance can actually backfire because it reinforces your underlying doubts and fears. It teaches you the unhelpful rule that the only way to cope is by avoiding things."

Living with low self-esteem can harm your mental health, leading to problems such as depression and anxiety. You may also develop unhelpful habits, such as smoking and drinking too much, as a way of coping.

How to have healthy self-esteem

In order to boost self-esteem, you need to identify and challenge the negative beliefs you have about yourself.

"You need to look at your beliefs, how you learned them and why you believe them," says Professor Williams. "Then actively begin to gather and write down evidence that disconfirms them."

Learn to spot the negative thoughts you have about yourself. You may tell yourself you are "too stupid" to apply for a new job, for example, or that "nobody cares" about you. Start to note these negative thoughts and write them down on a piece of paper or in a diary, suggests Professor Williams. Ask yourself when you first started to think these thoughts.

Next, start to write down evidence that challenges these negative beliefs: "I am really good at cryptic crosswords" or "My sister calls for a chat every week". Write down other positive things you know to be true about yourself, such as "I am thoughtful" or "I am a great cook" or "I am someone that others trust". Also write down good things that other people say about you.

Aim to have at least five things on your list and add to it regularly. Then put your list somewhere you can see it. That way, you can keep reminding yourself that you are OK.

"It's about helping people recognise they have strengths as well as weaknesses, like everyone else, and begin to recognise those strengths in themselves," says Professor Williams.

"You might have low confidence now because of what happened when you were growing up," he says. "But we can grow and develop new ways of seeing ourselves at any age."

Other ways to improve low self-esteem

Here are some other simple techniques that may help you feel better about yourself.

Recognise what you are good at

We are all good at something, whether it's cooking, singing, doing puzzles or being a friend. We also tend to enjoy doing the things we are good at, which can help to boost your mood.

Build positive relationships

If you find certain people tend to bring you down, try to spend less time with them, or tell them how you feel about their words or actions. Seek out relationships with people who are positive and who appreciate you.

Be kind to yourself

Professor Williams advises: "Be compassionate to yourself. That means being gentle to yourself at times when you feel like being self-critical. Think what you'd say to encourage a friend in a similar situation. We often give far better advice to others than we do to ourselves."

Learn to be assertive

Being assertive is about respecting other people's opinions and needs, and expecting the same from them.

One trick is to look at other people who act assertively and copy what they do. "It's not about pretending you're someone you're not," says Professor Williams. "It's picking up hints and tips from people you admire and letting the real you come out. There's no point suddenly saying, 'I'm going to be Chris Hoy', but you might be able to get your bike out and do a bit of cycling for the first time in ages."

Start saying 'no'

People with low self-esteem often feel they have to say yes to other people, even when they don't really want to. The risk is that you become overburdened, resentful, angry and depressed.

"For the most part, saying no doesn't upset relationships," says Professor Williams. "It can be helpful to take a scratched-record approach. Keep saying no in different ways until they get the message."

Give yourself a challenge

We all feel nervous or afraid to do things at times. People with healthy self-esteem don't let these feelings stop them from trying new things or taking on challenges.

Set yourself a goal, such as joining an exercise class or going to a social occasion. Achieving your goals will help to increase your self-esteem.

Where to find help for low self-esteem

You may feel you need some help to start seeing yourself in a more positive light. Talking therapies, such as counselling or cognitive behavioural therapy, can help. Your GP can explain the different types and tell you what's available in your area.

Read more about the different types of therapy

You can also refer yourself for counselling or therapy. Use the NHS Choices Services Directory or visit the British Association for Counselling & Psychotherapy website to find a registered counsellor and therapist near you.

24 September 2014

⇨ The above information is reprinted with kind permission from NHS Choices. Please visit www.nhs.uk for further information.

© NHS Choices 2016

To build children's character, leave self-esteem out of it

THE CONVERSATION

***An article from* The Conversation.**

By Kristján Kristjánsson, Professor of Character Education and Virtue Ethics Deputy Director, Jubilee Centre for Character and Virtues, University of Birmingham

In the last few months the UK's two main political parties have entered into an apparent bidding war over which of them can elevate the teaching of character highest on their educational agendas before the next general election.

With an extra flourish, the secretary of state for education, Nicky Morgan, announced a £3.5 million fund to "place character education on a par with academic learning" for pupils. This money will be spent on scaling-up existing initiatives and funding more research into character education.

This is good news. But a more worrying feature of the recent debate about character education is the apparent return of self-esteem and self-confidence as virtues to be cultivated at school.

In an article I wrote earlier this year for *The Conversation*, I warned against the unduly restrictive focus in character education on performance virtues, such as grit and resilience. This is being done at the expense of other character virtues – both moral, such as honesty and compassion, and intellectual, such as curiosity and love of learning. After all, who wants the resilience of the repeat offender?

Judging from recent coverage of debates around character education, this criticism is still valid in critiques of the views of character expressed both by Morgan, and Labour's shadow education secretary, Tristram Hunt.

That said, a closer look at the full text of Morgan's Priestley Lecture at the University of Birmingham and Hunt's speech at a recent joint Demos–Jubilee Centre conference reveals a more expansive view of character as both steadfastly laden with values and intrinsically important for a well-rounded, flourishing life.

Consciously building character

Some red herrings still survive in these waters. The terms "soft" and "non-cognitive" skills are relentlessly swirled around as designators of character virtues, at least of the performance kind. I hope this is just a language issue – politicians and journalists share a love of short and catchy phrases – because from an academic standpoint both terms are terrible misnomers.

Character traits are notoriously resistant to change, at least after middle to late childhood. There is a lot of truth in the words of Nobel Prize Laureate J M Coetzee that,

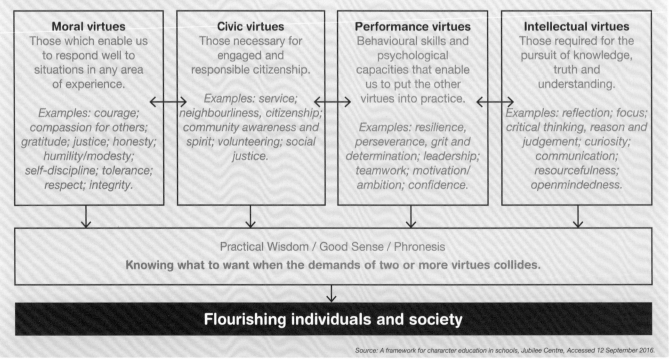

What is character education?

'[...] the ultimate aim of character education is the development of good sense or practical wisdom: the capacity to choose intelligently between alternatives.'

Moral virtues	Civic virtues	Performance virtues	Intellectual virtues
Those which enable us to respond well to situations in any area of experience.	Those necessary for engaged and responsible citizenship.	Behavioural skills and psychological capacities that enable us to put the other virtues into practice.	Those required for the pursuit of knowledge, truth and understanding.
Examples: courage; compassion for others; gratitude; justice; honesty; humility/modesty; self-discipline; tolerance; respect; integrity.	*Examples: service; neighbourliness, citizenship; community awareness and spirit; volunteering; social justice.*	*Examples: resilience, perseverance, grit and determination; leadership; teamwork; motivation/ ambition; confidence.*	*Examples: reflection; focus; critical thinking, reason and judgement; curiosity; communication; resourcefulness; openmindedness.*

Practical Wisdom / Good Sense / Phronesis
Knowing what to want when the demands of two or more virtues collides.

Flourishing individuals and society

Source: A framework for chararcter education in schools, Jubilee Centre, Accessed 12 September 2016.

after the skull, character is the second hardest part of the body.

In a similar vein, there is nothing non-cognitive about character virtues, even of the performance kind. For example, resilience is all about certain beliefs you harbour about your chances of overcoming adversity. All virtues, performance-driven, moral and intellectual, comprise a clear cognitive element.

Please, no comeback for self-esteem

When spelling out her priorities on character education, Morgan explained: "What I mean is a focus on things like the additional character skills we all need to get on in life – resilience, grit, self-esteem, self-confidence."

I thought self-esteem had been laid to rest as an educational aim after the famous meta-analysis by American psychologist Roy Baumeister and colleagues in 2003. It seems not. There were some salient findings from their research and from my further review of the 1990s' "self-concept" industry, focused on debates around self-esteem, self-confidence and self-respect.

These included that high general self-esteem is more pernicious than low self-esteem – it is more clearly connected to variables such as unprotected sex, bullying and experimenting with drugs. A likely explanation is that high self-esteem gives the person a false sense of invulnerability to negative consequences. Moderate and realistic self-esteem is, rather, the ideal psycho-moral state.

At the same time, while correlations have been found between self-esteem in maths and maths scores, the maths results are more likely to cause the self-esteem, rather than the other way around.

Who we are deep down

The return of debates around self-esteem and self-confidence is potentially more counter-productive for the character agenda than the focus on resilience – as almost no eminent social scientists take it seriously any more. To put it simply, character is much more about who we really are deep down rather than who we think we are.

It is heartening to see messages and findings from our work at the Jubilee Centre for Character and Virtues gradually filtering through to UK politicians. But, as yet, their faculty to express their new-found interest still lags slightly behind their enthusiasm for conveying the message that character matters for academic achievement and general human flourishing.

17 December 2014

⇨ The above information is reprinted with kind permission from *The Conversation*. Please visit www.theconversation.com for further information.

Children's confidence destroyed by social media

ChildLine says young people have been coming forward in their droves to confide just how desperate, alone and sad they feel.

By Paul Cardwell

The confidence of children living in Scotland is being destroyed by a constant onslaught from cyber-bullying and social media.

Marking its 30th anniversary, ChildLine said today's young people are finding it difficult to cope with the pressures of modern life, creating a generation plagued by loneliness and low self-esteem.

The counselling service said in 2014–15 it held 35,244 counselling sessions across the UK for children with low self-esteem, an increase of 9% from the previous year.

One of the biggest influences it said was social media and the desire to copy celebrities as they strive to achieve the "perfect" image.

One 13-year-old girl told counsellors the pressure to keep up with her peers had led her to hate herself and she rarely left her bedroom.

She said: "When I look at other girls online posting photos of themselves it makes me feel really worthless and ugly.

"I'm struggling to cope with these feelings and stay in my bedroom most of the time. I'm always worrying about what other people are thinking of me. I feel so down."

It's not just girls that are struggling though.

A 14-year-old boy told the service how lonely he felt.

He said: "I don't really have many friends in real life and spend a lot of time in my bedroom on my laptop.

"I don't have much confidence in myself and I feel as if my life is really depressing."

Peter Wanless, chief executive of NSPCC which operates ChildLine, said it was clear from the hundreds of thousands of calls it receives that we have a nation of deeply unhappy children.

He said: "The pressure to keep up with friends and have the perfect life online is adding to the sadness that many young people feel on a daily basis.

"The worries that young people face and the way they talk to us have dramatically changed since ChildLine was launched, and we will change to make sure that no matter what, young people will have a place to turn to whenever they need it."

Since its launch in 1986, ChildLine, which has centres in Aberdeen and Glasgow, has helped over four million children via its round the clock service.

Back at the beginning, children were mostly concerned about family planning problems and sexual abuse.

Children exclusively made contact by telephone – street corner boxes or home lines – or freepost letter but last year fewer than one in three counselling sessions took place via phone.

In fact, 71% of sessions involved one-to-one chat or email and last year was the third in a row that ChildLine has counselled more young people online than by phone, as the trend to reach out via the Internet continues.

Wanless added: "Times may change but one thing stays the same – our vital helpline is often the only place that many young people feel they can turn to."

7 January 2016

⇨ The above information is reprinted with kind permission from Third Force News. Please visit www.thirdforcenews.org.uk for further information.

Latest expensive must-have

Public rejection

Idealised body image

24 hour social media

Help!

Cyberbullying

Unrealistic expectations

Study finds physically active children are happier and more confident

Change4Life and Disney's 10 minute shake up campaign launches with release of new study on the benefits of physical activity for children.

2 July 2015 marked the launch of this year's 'Change4Life 10 minute shake up' campaign with Disney. The campaign aims to encourage children to do ten minute bursts of moderate to vigorous activity, inspired by Disney characters, throughout the day, and every day, in order to meet the recommended 60 minutes of physical activity children need.

This year's campaign launches to coincide with the publication of an evidence review by British Heart Foundation (BHF) researchers from the University of Oxford and Loughborough University, which identifies the direct benefits that physical activity has on children in terms of their physical, social and emotional development.

The new review points to strong evidence that physical activity and sport has a positive impact on children's social skills and self-esteem. The evidence review also identified further social benefits for children as a result of physical activity, including increased confidence and peer acceptance, alongside a link to friendship.

Review author Professor Charlie Foster commented:

"The positives of exercise on children's mental wellbeing are less well known than the physical benefits. The evidence showed a strong link between physically active children and improved self-esteem, confidence, attention span and even academic achievements."

Over a third of children in the UK are overweight, yet 79% of parents with an overweight child do not recognise that they are, and of those that do, 41% do not realise that it is a health risk. Furthermore, parents tend to overestimate how active their children are. Change4Life with Disney aims to inspire children to get active using Disney characters and stories as encouragement.

New for this year's campaign, the Change4Life 10 Minute Shake Up game allows kids to join one of four Disney teams: Frozen, Toy Story, Monsters and Big Hero 6 and help their team win by doing as many 'shake ups' as they can every day.

To mark today's campaign launch, Change4Life and Disney are hosting England's largest ever interactive PE lesson. An exclusive ten minute shake up will be available to schools from 9am on Thursday 2 July. The film stars Ricky Wilson, Kaiser Chiefs frontman and TV judge on *The Voice* who is also a keen runner and fitness enthusiast. Ricky will guide children through a ten minute shake up game inspired by the moves of Disney characters from the shake up teams.

This is the second year that Change4Life has teamed up with Disney. Last year's campaign resulted in the nation's kids being active for an extra 104 million minutes of the summer.

Professor Kevin Fenton, National Director of Health and Wellbeing at Public Health England (PHE), commented:

"Levels of childhood obesity are unacceptably high – currently one in five primary school children is overweight or obese. This latest review reinforces the essential health and wellbeing benefits of being physically active. Breaking up the 60 minutes of physical activity that children need each day into ten minute bursts will be more appealing and manageable for children and parents alike."

Public Health Minister, Jane Ellison, said:

"Exercise is really important for children, and it's vital that we encourage them to form healthy habits to last throughout their life.

"The 10 minute shake up programme is great for introducing children to manageable, bite-size chunks of activity – and, best of all, it's fun. With the summer holidays coming up, it's ideal for parents and children to get active together."

Marianthi O'Dwyer, Vice President and Head of Living Well at Disney UK and Ireland said:

Following on from the success of last year's campaign, we're excited to be partnering with Change4Life for a brand new ten minute shake up. This year children will have the chance to join one of four Disney-themed teams, which we hope will inspire them to get even more active this summer.

"Disney's stories are experienced and enjoyed by children around the world, so we believe we can have a positive influence. Our partnership with Change4Life is part of Disney's commitment to use our stories and characters to inspire and encourage life-long healthy behaviours in families."

2 July 2015

⇨ The above information is reprinted with kind permission from Public Health England. Please visit www.gov.uk for further information.

Key facts

- Positive body image occurs when a person is able to accept, appreciate and respect their body. (page 1)

- The *Dove Global Beauty and Confidence Report* found that women in the UK have one of the lowest body confidence scores in the world, with only 20% of us saying we like the way that we look. (page 4)

- Globally, more than two-thirds of women (69%) and girls (65%) say increasing pressures from advertising and media to reach an unrealistic standard of beauty is the key force in driving their appearance anxiety. (page 4)

- There is a gender split. Woman are far more likely to be unhappy with their body image. Over four in ten (44%) are not happy, compared to 53% who are. Men seem to be a little bit more comfortable in their own skin – 66% are happy compared to 31% that are not. (page 5)

- Does loving your body begin at 60? Certainly the sexagenarians in our poll liked their bodies more than other age groups. Almost seven in ten (68%) of 60+ are happy, compared to 52% of 25–39-year-olds. (page 5)

- Residents from Saudi Arabia (72%), Oman (70%) and Qatar (70%) are the next happiest with their body image overall. (page 5)

- In the UK, almost three quarters (74%) say that celebrity culture has a negative impact on women's perception of their bodies, while the same number say it affects young people in the same way. Overall, in 17 of the 25 countries surveyed more than half of responders think that celebrity culture has a negative impact on young people. (page 5)

- Recent figures show that 91% of teens have taken a selfie and over one million are taken each day. (page 6)

- Body dysmorphia can lead to distress, social anxiety, depression, self-harm and in some cases, suicide. (page 10)

- Recent research from YMCA revealed that 34% of teenage boys and 49% of teenage girls had been on a diet in an effort to change their body shape.(page 13)

- 33–35% of boys aged six to eight indicate their ideal body is thinner than their current body. (page 15)

- The measurements of the male action figures young boys play with exceed even those of the biggest bodybuilders. (page 15)

- French MPs pass a law making it illegal to employ unhealthily thin women or photoshop images without stating it clearly. (page 16)

- 87% of TV characters aged ten to 17 are below average in weight. (page 18)

- A record number of over 51,000 Britons underwent cosmetic surgery in 2015, demonstrating the public's love affair with surgical enhancement is far from over, despite any previous 'blips' as the economy reshaped itself. (page 20)

- Although men still account for just 9% of the total number of cosmetic surgery operations in the UK, their numbers have nearly doubled over the past decade (from 2,440 procedures in 2005 to 4,614 in 2015). (page 18)

- From the moment of birth, our self-esteem begins to take shape by what others think about us and how we are treated. Family members and caregivers are powerful influences on shaping our early self-esteem. (page 29)

- Results show that most kids develop a sense of self-esteem – feeling good or bad about oneself – as early as age five, before they even enter kindergarten. (page 33)

- In 2014–15 ChildLine said it held 35,244 counselling sessions across the UK for children with low self-esteem, an increase of 9% from the previous year. One of the biggest influences it said was social media and the desire to copy celebrities as they strive to achieve the "perfect" image. (page 38)

- Over a third of children in the UK are overweight, yet 79% of parents with an overweight child do not recognise that they are, and of those that do, 41% do not realise that it is a health risk. (page 39)

Airbrushing

A technique used to edit photos. Airbrushing may involve the removal of blemishes or spots, changing the shape or size of a person's features, and may lighten a person's skin tone. These digital edits are usually done in a way to make the final effect appear natural.

BMI (body mass index)

An abbreviation which stands for 'body mass index' and is used to determine whether an individual's weight is in proportion to their height. If a person's BMI is below 18.5 they are usually seen as being underweight. If a person has a BMI greater than or equal to 25, they are classed as overweight and a BMI of 30 and over is obese. As BMI is the same for both sexes and adults of all ages, it provides the most useful population-level measure of overweight and obesity. However, it should be considered a rough guide because it may not correspond to the same degree of 'fatness' in different individuals (e.g. a body builder could have a BMI of 30 but would not be obese because his weight would be primarily muscle rather than fat).

Body Dysmorphic Disorder (BDD)

A mental health condition where a person has an excessive concern over their body image and what they perceive as their 'flaws'.

Body image

Body image is the subjective sense we have of our appearance and the experience of our physical embodiment. It is an individual's perception of what they look like or how they should look like. It can be influenced by personal memory along with external sources such as the media and comments made by other people

Cosmetic surgery

A medical procedure which changes a person's appearance and can be performed on most parts of the human body. Cosmetic surgery can involve procedures such as inputting breast implants, bum lifts, Botox and lip fillers as well as changing bone structure.

Eating disorder

A term used to describe a range of psychological disorders that involve disturbed eating habits such as anorexia or bulimia nervosa.

Objectify/Objectification

To turn something into an object in relation to sight, touch or another physical sense. To 'objectify' a person means to turn them into an object, meaning that they do not possess the same human rights as another individual. The person objectified is usually dominated by another person, or group of people.

Photoshop

A term applied to photos which are edited using digital software, and usually refers to editing which is done using the computer programme Adobe Photoshop. Airbrushing is one technique which may be used when 'photoshopping' an image.

Self-esteem

A term referring to how an individual feels about their body. Relating to self-confidence, if a person has low self-esteem they may feel unhappy with the way they look. Alternatively, if a person has good/high self-esteem then they may feel particularly confident about their appearance.

Selfie

The selfie has become a huge part of modern life. A selfie is a photograph that a person takes of themselves, usually with a smartphone or digital camera, usually with the intent of sharing it on social media. It has transformed the simple self-portrait into something more immediate and has grown in cultural importance – it's been linked to identity, self-exploration and narcissism.

Size-zero

A term referring to U.S. clothing, size-zero is equivalent to a UK size-four. In order to fit into size-zero clothing an individual must have the waist measurement of 23 inches which is the average waist size of an eight-year-old.

Assignments

Brainstorming

⇨ In small groups, discuss what you know about body confidence.

- What is body image?
- What is self-esteem?
- What is a selfie?
- What does the term 'photoshopping' mean?

Research

⇨ Write an article on the issues surrounding the possible impact that social media has upon body image and self-esteem. You should conduct some online research on the topic, investigating how viable this claim may be, as well finding evidence to support your conclusions.

⇨ What is Body Dysmorphic Disorder (BDD)? Create a PowerPoint presentation explaining what BDD is and the effect it can have on someone's life.

⇨ Read *Nine body positive social media campaigns that are changing how we perceive beauty both in and outside the fashion world* on page 17 and select one positive social media campaign to research further (or choose one of your own).

⇨ "Recent figures show that 91% of teens have taken a selfie and over one million are taken each day." Take a survey of your family, friends and classmates and find out if anyone has ever taken a selfie before. If so, how often do they take selfies? Do they ever alter their selfies? Why do they take selfies? Compile all your data into graphs and present your findings to the class.

Design

⇨ In small groups, design an app for a smartphone that will highlight the body image issues that teenagers today are facing. Your app should also offer help and advice on tackling these issues.

⇨ Produce a poster using the statistics surrounding body image issues found throughout this book. You may also find the *Key facts* section useful (page 40).

⇨ Produce a leaflet which raises awareness about the dangers surrounding eating disorders such as anorexia nervosa, bulimia nervosa and binge-eating disorders.

⇨ Choose one of the articles from this book and create an illustration that highlights the key themes of the piece.

⇨ Create a music playlist of songs to help boost someone's confidence and self-esteem when they're feeling down. You can also include positive quotes, books or even activities that help build confidence and boost self-esteem (e.g. dancing, playing sports, etc.). You might want to include a reason as to why you selected a certain piece.

Oral

⇨ Create a storyboard for a YouTube video explaining how airbrushing and Photoshop alter photographs. You should provide examples of digitally enhanced photos which are circulated by the media and you should discuss how these edited photographs may affect members of the public who see them.

⇨ In pairs, discuss whether you think the Government is doing enough to tackle body image issues is children and teens. What else could they do? Does your school discuss these issues with you? Do you think they should? Make notes on your discussion and feedback to your class.

⇨ Hold a class discussion on body image to discover which concerns directly affect you and your fellow students. You may want to consider how images circulated in the media affect your self-confidence or consider whether any of the statistics found in this book are also applicable to your perception of yourself.

⇨ In pairs, go through this book and discuss the cartoons you come across. Think about what the artists were trying to portray with each illustration.

Reading/writing

⇨ Imagine you are an Agony Aunt writing for a national newspaper. A young girl has written to you admitting that she has self-esteem and body confidence issues. Write a suitable reply giving advice and information on where she may look for support in order to tackle her concerns.

⇨ Do you think male body issues receive as much media coverage and are as readily discussed as female body issues? Give reasons for your answer and consider which issues are frequently discussed for both genders, and/or what needs to be more discussed in your opinion.

⇨ Read *France divides the fashion world by banning skinny models* on page 16. Summarise the article and include your own thoughts on the topic. Do you agree with this law? Why or why not?

⇨ "A record number of over 51,000 Britons underwent cosmetic surgery in 2015." – The British Associations of Aesthetic Plastic Surgeons (BAAPS). Write an essay about what plastic/cosmetic surgery is: you might want to include its history and what procedures people have done and why.

Acknowledgements

The publisher is grateful for permission to reproduce the material in this book. While every care has been taken to trace and acknowledge copyright, the publisher tenders its apology for any accidental infringement or where copyright has proved untraceable. The publisher would be pleased to come to a suitable arrangement in any such case with the rightful owner.

Images

All images courtesy of iStock.

All icons are made by Freepik from www.flaticon.com, except the bowls on page 3 © Madebyoliver, the sad face on page 18 © Chanut is Industries and page 41 © SimpleIcon.

Illustrations

Don Hatcher: pages 9 & 35. Simon Kneebone: pages 2 & 27. Angelo Madrid: pages 17 & 38.

Additional acknowledgements

Editorial on behalf of Independence Educational Publishers by Cara Acred.

With thanks to the Independence team: Mary Chapman, Sandra Dennis, Christina Hughes, Jackie Staines and Jan Sunderland.

Cara Acred

Cambridge

September 2016